cans
d the
ped Wire

Americans Behind the Barbed Wire

WORLD WAR II: INSIDE A GERMAN PRISON CAMP

J. FRANK DIGGS

VANDAMERE PRESS

Published by
Vandamere Press
P.O. Box 5243
Arlington, VA 22205

Copyright 2000
Vandamere Press

ISBN 0~918339~52~9

Contents

Foreword

It might seem strange to start a book that is going to deal with a military aspect of World War II by talking about consumer economics in the 1930s. However, the economic climate in the United States during the decade before the war was, I believe, key to making possible much of the action in this book. This climate had the most to do with forming the character of the Americans who fought in that war, thereby helping to create a tough and resourceful American fighting man.

America in the 1930s was experiencing the effects of the worst financial crisis since the Civil War. The result yielded a generation of young men who had faced a reality rarely seen before or since that time. They learned to work hard and cope with adversity of many kinds. The depression that began in 1929 lasted until the early phases of World War II and created a different country than we have today.

Unemployment in that period rose rapidly from 3.2 percent to 24.9 percent. Everyone had to work harder and overcome difficult situations in order to survive. Even after nearly a decade of depression and drastic measures instituted by the Roosevelt New Deal, 17.1 percent of Americans remained unemployed. No safety net existed as we know it today. More than 80 percent of U.S. families, or 21.5 million households, had no savings at all to fall back on. Incomes dropped by 29 percent and people learned to rely more and more on one another and their own ingenuity.

For those lucky enough to have jobs, pay cuts soon became a fact of life. Cuts of 10 percent or much more became common, then universal. Men who worked on Works Projects Administration (WPA) jobs were paid just $5 a day, women $3. In New York City, live-in maids earned less than $8 a week and felt lucky to have a place to live. These conditions had a profound effect on the young men growing up in the 10 years before the war. The famed economist, Robert S. McElvaine, summed it up very well when he wrote:

"The hardships many families faced in the thirties led children to assume greater responsibilities at an earlier age than has been customary in the years since World War II. It has been said with some accuracy that there were no working-class 'teenagers' in the 1930s. That generation had no time for an irresponsible prolonged adolescence. Challenges had to be met. Often children—especially boys—were called upon to support meager family incomes by working after school or in place of school. . . .

"There were some compensations for the youth in the thirties, however. The work thrust upon the children was likely to to install in them what industrial society commonly considers to be virtues: dependability, self-reliance, order, awareness of the needs of others, and practice in the management of money. . . . Ironically, the same family hardships that might weaken the self-reliance of a father could strengthen the quality of the child."[1]

Life in America before the depression was far harder than today, but after the depression set in, the difference between then and now was harder even for those who had jobs and were able to get along on reduced incomes. No conveniences existed such as air conditioners, television sets, frozen dinners, automatic dishwashers, videocassettes, computers, or other things that make life today so much easier. Also, no Social Security, Medicare, or food stamps were available to fall back on when things went wrong. People had to rely on one another to a much greater extent; family and friends became more important. In spite of all their economic troubles, people remained proud of their country and willing to make sacrifices for it.

The Americans of that day, those who fought in World War II, came from a different mix of people, too. It was a smaller country with a population perhaps

---

[1]Robert S. Mcelvaine. *The Great Depression: America 1929-1941.* Times Books.

half of what it is today. It was composed mostly of people of European ancestry, the English and the Germans predominating. Only a few Latinos were found except in the southwest. The only visible Asiatics were operating popular laundries or Chinese restaurants. Blacks were segregated to an almost unbelievable extent. In the Army you found only all-black units with white officers, and then only in non-combat roles. Before the war, no women were admitted into the Army at all, except as nurses or civilian employees.

Like most other junior officers in World War II, I had been strongly affected by the depression. My father was an engineer, and a good one, with a responsible position in Baltimore County, Maryland. But when the cutback came in the depression, he lost his job early on and spent years trying to find another one. He even tried selling life insurance, but never successfully. We moved back to an old family home in Linthicum Heights, Maryland, to save rent, but I never found out how the family continued to eat regularly.

When the time came to go to college, there was no money in the till. Fewer than 10 percent of high school graduates were able to finance college in those days. By sheer good fortune however, and the fact I had been editor of my high school paper, I obtained a full scholarship at the American University (AU) in Washington, D.C. No ROTC existed, to my slight disappointment, but I did become editor of the college paper, *The American Eagle*, which paid a stipend of $100 a semester, thus helping with my food bill.

As an example of how young college students survived in those days, I took a variety of part-time jobs to pay for room and board. I was a waiter in the college dining room and a substitute classroom janitor. On weekends, I would become an outdoor waiter at the local Hot Shoppes hamburgery, with no pay but lots of nickel-and-dime tips. Sometimes I would get a much-sought-after job of wrapping and mailing a Washington newsletter published by the Bureau of National Affairs. My best job by far, acquired in the summer of my junior year, was as the driver of a Good Humor truck which paid a munificent salary that averaged about $25 a week, based on sales. The only drawback was the hours: 12 hours a day, 7 days a week, or about 100 hours a week. Fortunately, it was fun and I saved enough to purchase, among other things, a fine, secondhand sports car for $75, a '29 Nash that greatly improved my social life for my last year at AU.

In 1938, the day after I graduated and just a year before Hitler began his rampage across Europe, I offered my services to *The Washington Post*. I was lucky enough to get the only opening available, that of a lowly copy boy at $15 a week. I stayed with the *Post* for three years, rising gradually to reporting feature stories, covering press conferences and writing a weekly column about the citizens' associations which then substituted for democracy in Washington. I shared a nice, third-floor walk-up apartment with Dillard Stokes, the *Post's* legal reporter, for which we each paid $22 a month. I also met a lovely young government girl, named Tracy, at an Oklahoma State Society dance. I attended the dance with one of the free tickets that arrived on the city desk quite often. It was a good life, even if money was short.

As the war was drawing near, Congress passed—by one vote—a peacetime draft law that called for all qualified young men from 21 years to 36 years to serve for one year in the Army. It turned out to be the start of a massive draft of 10 million American men from 18 to 45 into the armed services for the duration of World War II. In 1940 the U.S. Army needed men badly; it was down to token strength. I was clearly eligible, as a young fellow, 23 years old , healthy and single. When my call came, I had reason for one delay: I had been taking graduate work at George Washington University and was within sight of a master's degree in economics. I had just finished my master's thesis, "Industrial Unionization of the Building Trades in Washington, D.C." when I asked for, and was granted, a two-month deferment. However, I was told to report for military duty in May 1941. Actually, I was not at all reluctant to spend a year in the Army. I liked to travel a bit and could enjoy some healthy outdoor living.

So that May I took my physical, passed it, packed a small suitcase, had a farewell drink with my friends at the National Press Club, said goodbye to Tracy, and went off to join the U.S. Army as a new draftee.

Americans
Behind the
Barbed Wire

Captured

1

It was pitch black outside. We were sailing with lights out across the Mediterranean as part of the largest invasion fleet ever assembled up to that time. The time was July, 1943, and I had been in the Army for just over two years, half of that time as a junior officer. We were headed for Sicily with 3,000 ships of all kinds, 160,000 American and British troops, 14,000 vehicles and 600 tanks. Our landing destination was at Licata on the southern coast of the island, while the British were to land on the east coast. We had six divisions, the British had seven.

Sailing from North Africa, where we had spent the winter since the landing at Casablanca, my battalion of the 3rd Division embarked aboard a landing ship-tank (LST), for the overnight trip to Sicily. We had little or no sleep on the crowded landing ship that night. Just before dawn, we began to unload onto smaller landing craft when the enemy artillery started to fire at the convoy. The enemy fire was almost constant as we moved toward the Sicilian coast. Our Navy responded by firing over our heads at the shore installations. Some of our small landing craft were hit, far too many, but mine was not.

Somehow, we got ashore, even with the German artillery still blasting away. The Germans obviously knew we were coming. The first men ashore were soon able to silence the shore batteries and we pushed inland. None of my men were hit, thank God. It turned out that the British forces got the worst of it, landing on the east coast where two German divisions were waiting to greet them. Once ashore, our U.S. invasion force met only sporadic opposition as we moved partway across the island the first day.

Then my battalion, in the lead, ran up against a well-entrenched enemy blockade of indeterminate size. The colonel looked at young Lieutenant Diggs and said, "See what you can do." So my platoon was elected. I spread them out to look like a much larger force. I then told a German-speaking corporal in the platoon to shout out, in German and Italian, "You are surrounded—raise up a white flag and surrender!" as we crept around the flank. By now we were getting heavy enemy fire. We moved slowly forward for about 3,000 yards of broken ground, firing everything we had. Then the enemy firing ceased and, much to my surprise, a white flag was raised. About 150 enemy troops, most of them Italian, stood up and surrendered. A few of them had been hit; none of my men had. That action ended the roadblock and the battalion moved on ahead. I discovered much later after I had been captured that this action had earned me a much-coveted silver star medal, which was presented to my wife Tracy at a ceremony in Baltimore, in my absence.

After about a month of the Sicilian campaign, the Americans and British had driven across the island to Palermo. The remaining two German armored divisions were withdrawing along the northern coast toward Messina. Their objective was to evacuate Sicily and set up a strong German defense in Italy. It was at this point that General George Patton had one of his less brilliant ideas: to land one of his best amphibious battalions in front of the retreating Germans to see if they would surrender to a smaller American force. General Omar Bradley, then on Patton's staff, told him not to persist in this plan, that it was a foolhardy idea that would unnecessarily cost a lot of American casualties.[1] But, of course, Patton went ahead with it.

My battalion was chosen to implement Patton's plan, so we loaded up on landing craft Infantry (LCIs) and sailed out one night, to land at dawn somewhere along the coast where our intelligence sources thought the Germans might be. As it turned out, the German divisions had already passed this point, and we

---

[1] General Omar N. Bradley, *A Soldier's Story*. New York: Holt.

were able to cut off just a small piece of their tail. "Let's do it again and get it right this time," Patton said.

So we geared up to make our fourth amphibious landing, hoping that this one would not be under fire. This time, we sailed overnight in an LST, big enough for the whole battalion, and went ashore in small landing craft just before dawn. Searchlights from shore located us but there was no artillery fire, so we landed quietly in the darkness near the small Sicilian town of Brollo. The colonel led most of the battalion up the mountains to positions overlooking the coast. He ordered me and my platoon to block the coastal road with the help of some self-propelled howitzers loaned to us by the 1st Armored Corps and commanded by Lt. Martin Keiser.

We dug in to cover the coastal road. Then came the Germans, first with jeeps and trucks which we stopped with rifle fire and the howitzers. Soon there-after came the big German tanks with 88-mm canons, which proceeded to knock out our howitzers, one by one. German sharp-shooters appeared out of nowhere, aiming at my platoon and killing two good men before we knew what was happening. This action went on all day. We actually held up the German with-drawal for 12 hours before their tanks broke through and German troops poured over my position. I told those who could make it to go up the mountain to join the battalion's position and most of them did. A few of us were wounded—including myself with some shrapnel in my leg—and were knocked out before we could follow, so we were overrun and captured.[2]

Becoming a prisoner of war turned out to be very matter of fact. A German soldier helped me to my feet and escorted me and Lt. Keiser to a German com-mand car, which drove us, together with two other captured officers through the darkness to the eastern end of the island. Thus, I became a prisoner of war, a POW, the last thing I ever expected to be.

We arrived at the Straits of Messina at about midnight and were transferred to one of dozens of small boats that were engaged in evacuating the German divi-sions from Sicily. I remember that it was very noisy going across the straits to Italy with much artillery fire coming from someplace and American airplanes attack-ing the evacuation boats. None of this fire seemed to be doing any damage to any

---

[2]After the war, Lt. Diggs found he had been awarded a Bronze Star and a Purple Heart for that action.

of the boats that I could see. This time I was glad that the allied aim was not always effective.

Once on the Italian side of the straits, we four American prisoners were driven to a POW camp somewhere south of Naples, where a somber German doctor treated my leg and assured me that the wound was minor. This camp had contained many American and British troops taken prisoner in North Africa, but was now largely vacant. Here we had our first introduction to German prison fare. It was pretty bad and in short supply, or so I thought at the time. There was little to do except talk to each other, which we did.

A few days later, a German officer called the four of us together and issued the strangest invitation I had ever heard. We were being invited to have dinner with the two-star commanding general of the German 2nd Armored Division, which had been our nemesis in Sicily. An unbelievable, but real, invitation, and of course there was no declining such an offer. So that evening we four American and one Australian officer sat down at a long table under a large oak tree, together with the German general and eight or ten officers from his staff. Dinner came, a chicken dish of some kind. Then the general addressed us in perfect English. It seems that he wanted our views, as allied officers, on a purely hypothetical matter: Would there be any way in which two civilized countries like Germany and the United States, and possibly England, could come to some agreement to stop fighting each other and join forces to fight our common enemy—the Godless, communist country of Russia?

Our answer, of course, was couched in diplomatic terms but in effect we said something like "Never, at least not with Hitler still running Germany." The general apparently expected that answer, but thanked us anyway and bade us good evening, sending us back to the camp with some welcome leftover chicken.

After two or three weeks at the Italian camp, half a dozen of us, American officer POWs, were sent by truck to Rome. Then we were put aboard a regular passenger train in a guarded compartment and shipped off to Germany. This was the first and only comfortable trip we would ever make as POWs. That night, while the train was moving slowly through the Brenner Pass in the Alps, one of our group—a savvy New Yorker named Capt. Richard Rossback—managed to pry open a window and jump out. This escape caused great consternation among the German guard detail the next morning, and it probably marked the end of passenger train travel for Germany's war prisoners. Rossback got away unhurt, but he was later turned in by unfriendly Italians and recaptured by the Germans. He rejoined us a few months later.

In another prison camp just outside Berlin we learned a little about the German technique for interrogating prisoners—at least American prisoners. About a dozen U.S. officers were brought in and each placed in solitary confinement for a period of several weeks. I was kept in a tiny room with a small window up near the ceiling, a cot, and a a small wooden desk. Two meals, consisting mostly of cabbage soup, were brought in each day by a Russian POW. I found the boredom worse than expected and did everything I could think of to occupy my mind. I even tried to recall details of everything I had learned at graduate school, which didn't help much. The boredom grew worse, not better, as I ran out of good things to remember.

Every day or two, I would be escorted to an interrogation room and questioned by a solemn young German who spoke American-style English. He wanted to know obvious things about the new weapons my division was using and where the Americans were planning to invade France. There was no torture or even threat of torture, at least as far as I was concerned, even though I couldn't give any answers except for my name, rank and serial number. He was persistent, however, and when he found how badly I missed cigarettes he gave me one—but without a match to smoke it with. Some of my colleagues who were with armored units came under more pressure and were kept in solitary longer. At one point, a young English-speaking soldier was admitted to my cell and said he was a Canadian prisoner. He made light conversation and then asked oblique questions about the latest weapons used by the 3rd Division. He was obviously a phony. He didn't know the capital of Canada for one thing, so I dismissed him forthwith.

Eventually I was released from solitary and quartered with seven or eight other American lieutenants who had been captured earlier. I well remember Lt. Larry Phelan, a tall, soft-spoken New Jerseyite, giving me my first cigarette—along with a light—in three weeks, badly needed at the time. He reported that the camp also housed many Russian prisoners who were treated abominably. One time, when the Germans turned loose a fierce guard dog in their compound, the dog quickly disappeared. His bare bones were later thrown back over the barbed wire.

When our group of POWs had completed its interrogation, we were trucked into Berlin and then taken by subway under guard to a large railway station. I well remember seeing a small group of obviously Jewish men standing under guard in that station, awaiting their fate. In Berlin we found that our days of first-class travel were over as the door to our crowded boxcar slid closed. That began a long, stop-and-go trip across northern Germany and Poland, without food, water, or other comforts. Our destination, we found out later, was the small Polish town of Schubin, where we were to be introduced to our new home as prisoners of the Nazi Germans.

This is the Army . . .

2 On the long ride by freight car from Berlin to the officers' prison camp in northern Poland, I had plenty of time to ponder how I had landed in this damnable situation, a prisoner of war of the unpredictable Germans. It had started more than two years earlier, in 1941, when I was a new draftee in the United States, taking a much more comfortable passenger train from Washington, D.C., to Fort Bliss, located just outside El Paso, Texas. There I was assigned to a former National Guard unit from Washington, D.C. that had been activated a few months earlier. That summer was devoted to basic training in the arid heat of west Texas, a fairly rugged experience, but I had sort of enjoyed it. When the captain heard that I had two degrees in economics, he figured that I must know how to use a typewriter, hence I became the company clerk.

One Sunday afternoon in December, I was working on some files in the company tent when somebody came running in and yelled that we were being attacked at Pearl Harbor, wherever that was. I told him where it was, reported the attack to the captain, and then watched the army pull itself together.

Things moved quickly after that. A train appeared miraculously that evening, with flat cars for our 360th Coast Artillery AA guns and passenger cars for the troops. We packed hurriedly and most of us took off for a last evening at Jaurez, across the Rio Grande in Mexico.

As a new draftee in 1941 a few months before Pearl Harbor, I was issued a World War I helmet. Here I am shown wearing it during target practice at Fort Bliss, Texas.

Our former National Guard unit had been ordered to the West Coast to cope with a possible Japanese invasion there. We left the next morning and in three days we were in Seattle. Of course, the expected invasion never occurred. Our unit was then moved to Fort Lawton, just outside the city.

The war was on and America was in it. The damage done to our Navy at Pearl Harbor was severe. Where would the Japanese attack next? Alaska and the chain of Aleutian islands seemed logical targets. Thus, after guarding Seattle for two weeks, we were ordered aboard an old Alaska Steamship Lines freighter that had been converted into a troop ship. We were told that we would be escorting a bunch of recruits to man the Aleutians. As a corporal at the time, I was put in charge of a small 37-mm antitank gun on the bow of the ship and given a squad of men to use in firing back at any enemy submarines that might attack us. The gun seemed to me to be a very minimal defense against any determined submarine, but it was all that was available and we practiced firing it a few times.

We sailed up the beautiful inside passage from Seattle to the Gulf of Alaska and managed to run into the worst storm at sea I have ever seen. The old ship listed 30 degrees or more. Everyone was seasick. By Christmas, we reached Seward, left some troops there in the grim darkness of an Alaskan winter, and sailed on to Dutch Harbor and Unalaska. I had never seen a more desolate place, with no trees or vegetation, no towns, and miserable, cold, damp weather. We unloaded the rest of our troops, then happily sailed back to Seattle. Fortunately, there were no submarines to be seen, coming or going.

I repeated this trip three times, delivering mostly recruits to various Aleutian Islands, before my application for Officer Candidate School (OCS) came through. Then I entrained for Fort Benning, Georgia, home of the Army's huge Infantry School. There I was assigned to OCS Class 64, one of the first to train the new draftees to become officers. It was a three-month course—a very rough one conducted in the superheated summer of 1942.

Officer training at Benning had been well thought out during the years before the war, and it included a little bit of everything. There were hands-on demonstrations of U.S. Army weapons, infantry tactics and troop-handling procedures, combined with a great many lectures on topics such as map-reading and staff work. There was also a lot of marching to various areas, climbing over things and much athletic activity. The officer candidates had no time for KP, so the food preparation and serving were done by local black

When war began, I was shipped to Seattle, then assigned as a new corporal to take draftees to Alaska and the Aleutians. I made four trips on this route, most of them pleasant, aboard an old freighter converted to serve as a troop carrier.

service troops. Despite the Army's complete segregation rule, incidentally, there were three or four black members in our OCS class, all of them outstanding officer material. I assumed they would be used later to officer all-black companies.

It was a rigorous three-months officer training course and we all lost weight. Suddenly it was all over and we pinned on our gold bars as second lieutenants. I bought my officer's uniforms and headed home with two whole weeks of leave ahead to look up my old friend Tracy.

My family debated at length about whether it was wise to get married just before I left to go overseas. But Tracy and I decided to marry and we did, in my family's living room in Linthicum Heights, presided over by the local Methodist minister. My father, who was now working for the War Department's Chief of Engineers, drove us to the B & O station in Baltimore afterwards and we took the train for Philadelphia. I remember a nice, middle-aged gentleman on the train who treated us to cocktails and wished us a happy marriage and a good war. He was half correct, anyhow. Our brief honeymoon lasted for three days at the old Ben Franklin Hotel in Philadelphia. We even worked in some sight-seeing at Independence Hall and the Liberty Bell. Then I was off to join the war.

My orders were to join the 3rd Infantry Division at a post somewhere down in Virginia. I took my bride with me and discovered that the division would be moving out in less than three weeks. After checking in with my battalion commander, a stern, able lieutenant colonel, I located a scarce room for Tracy while I moved into the Bachelor Officers Quarters on post.

It was a hectic two weeks getting ready to go overseas on what was billed as a major military operation. The 3rd Division was a fine, old-line Regular Army outfit with a great record in World War I and plans to expand it in this one. The division had just arrived from a training post in California and was practicing to conduct a big amphibious landing operation. Among other things, we were training every day to climb down "scramble nets" off the side of a big ship onto small landing craft that would carry about 30 men ashore under fire. It sounded simple, but it was far more difficult to do while carrying a fully loaded knapsack and a rifle, especially when high waves made it hard to jump into the small landing craft. We learned to do it, however, without many casualties and I got to know the young men I would be leading.

For the last few nights, I was able to smuggle Tracy into the Bachelor Quarters in place of my lieutenant roommate, who agreed to disappear somewhere overnight. A few other married officers did the same, which created something of a traffic jam at the bathrooms, where guards had to be stationed to warn resident officers when the head was in use by the ladies. One colonel was overheard to say, "Women, women everywhere—what is the Army coming to!"

Then in October 1942 the whole division moved out to the Navy Yard at Hampton Roads outside of Norfolk, where ships of a large convoy were forming up. As we boarded our troop ship, the word was that we were headed for a landing somewhere in North Africa to establish a foothold for a later invasion of Hitler's Europe. This rumor proved to be correct.

Off we sailed on a crowded troop ship across the Atlantic, as part of the first major military offensive by U.S. forces in the war. About 500 warships and 350 transports were involved, sailing from Norfolk, Ireland, and England. They were to converge on three ports in North Africa—Casablanca, Oran, and Algiers. Our convoy, escorted by several naval vessels, took 15 days to reach the African coast. The weather was fine all the way. All went well until we were within sight of the coast of French Morocco the last night. Then, with no lights showing, our blacked-out troopship was nearly rammed by a French freighter. Last-minute sounding of our ship's horn prevented that, however. Just before dawn, a recorded address by President Roosevelt in French was blasted out over the convoy's loudspeaker system, saying that we came in peace and would be landing shortly to help the French people defeat their German invaders. It may have helped; I don't know.

The mission of the 3rd Division was to take the French fort just outside Casablanca, known to be manned by Vichy French troops. Would they fight? No one knew for sure. Still in darkness, we climbed down the scramble nets onto our small landing craft and headed for the fortress. Then, shore batteries from the fort opened up, firing on the assault boats as they approached the shore. An immobilized French battleship also began to hurl 15-inch shells at the convoy, but it was soon taken out by dive bombers flying out of Gibraltar. My platoon's landing craft was not hit, but it got hung up on a sandbar about 30 feet from the shore. We were unable to reach land and the firing began to get closer, so we did the only thing we could do—we waded ashore in water up to our necks, one man at a time, carrying our weapons and knapsacks over our heads. Everybody made it. We joined in storming the French fort.

By the time we broke into the fort, its artillery had ceased firing and the French troops manning the guns had emerged looking grim and uncertain. Despite all the firing, only one of the men in my company was wounded in the battle, and the fort was surrendered properly. One French plane swooped over in an apparent attempt to strafe us, but the battle for Casablanca was over. We dug in and waited to see what the remaining 14 Vichy French divisions might do.

Operation Torch, as the landings were called, was reported to be "a phenomenal tactical and strategic success."[1] Within three weeks, 185,000 men, 20,000 vehicles and 200,000 tons of military supplies were safely landed ashore at three places in North Africa. At Oran, the U.S. 34th Infantry Division convoyed in from its training base in Ireland. At Algiers, the 1st Infantry Division and part of the 1st Armored met stiffer resistance. And at Casablanca, the 3rd Infantry

---

[1]Louis L. Snyder. *The War: A Concise History,* 1939–1945. Julian Messner, Inc.

Division had the most opposition. Soon the French divisions based in Africa agreed to join in and forget their allegiance to the Vichy government.

This experience in North Africa was my first as an officer in combat. It was also the first, and easiest, of four amphibious landings under fire that I was to participate in. After the Casablanca landing, our entire battalion climbed aboard an old French 40-and-8 freight train—designed for 40 men or 8 horses in World War I—and rode half-way across Morocco to the little Arab town of Guercif. Here our assignment was to stand by to stop Rommel's famed *Afrika Korps* in case they decided to make an end run around the allied forces in Tunisia. We set up tents and spent the winter doing training exercises. Occasionally there was an alert and we marched off across the desert looking for the rumored enemy. Fortunately, there never was one. Mostly we lived in complete isolation; it was frustrating and boring.

After three months in Morocco, we entrained again February 1943 and headed for Tunisia. There, all hell was breaking loose. German tanks had broken through Faid Pass in central Tunisia and inflicted, in nine days that month, what became the greatest land defeat on U.S. forces in history up to that time. More than 5,000 American soldiers were listed as casualties: 192 killed, 2,625 wounded and 2,459 captured or missing.[2] With the German breakthrough, more than 2,500 American infantrymen were trapped and encircled. Tanks of our crack 1st Armored division were ordered out to their rescue, but it was an impossible to carry out against what turned out to be two German *panzer* divisions. As a result, a U.S. armored battalion was all but wiped out. One infantry regiment was totally destroyed. Other units were decimated for equally obscure reasons. The American general in charge of this intelligence fiasco was send home shortly thereafter.

Soon cooler heads prevailed. My division, the 3rd, was part of a larger force of American and British troops that hit Rommel's force from the north, while Gen. Montgomery's Eighth British Army struck from the south. With little combat involved on the part of my unit, the German *Korps* surrendered. Rommel, of course, escaped to fight again.

---

[2]Ibid.

With Africa safely behind us, we began preparations for the massive invasion of Sicily, in the course of which the war was going to get remarkably hotter for me.

All of this was going through my mind during the long boxcar ride, after my capture, from Berlin to a Germans prison camp deep inside Poland. Now to get back to what lay ahead at that fearsome camp, established by the Nazis for American ground force officers.

A Unique Prison Camp

3 Arriving at the little Polish town of Schubin, we as new POWs climbed down from our German boxcar and marched along cobblestone streets to the town's main thoroughfare, *Adolph Hitler Strasse*, and along it to our new camp, Oflag 64. It did not look much like a prison camp. It had been, in fact, the campus of a boys' school and still looked like one, with some large, old buildings and even a few trees. However, there was no mistaking the two double 15-foot-high barbed wire fences that went around the 10-acre compound, nor the ominous-looking guard towers spotted at intervals around the enclosure, sporting large searchlights and machine guns. Between the double fences, perhaps 10 feet apart, were rolls of rusty barbed wire, which made escape over the fences look very unlikely.

I hobbled through the main gate and got my first look at Oflag 64. The name was short for *Offizierlager*, or Officers' Camp— the Germans' special prison camp for American ground-force officers. Just inside the double gate was the old, original classroom building, a three-story structure now used for dormitories and offices for the senior American officer, or SAO. Next to it was a crude wooden latrine, large enough for maybe 50 men to use at a time. Nearby was the camp hospital, a two-story affair with 30 to 35 beds for badly wounded prisoners and others who had succumbed to problems of limited diet or cold Polish weather.

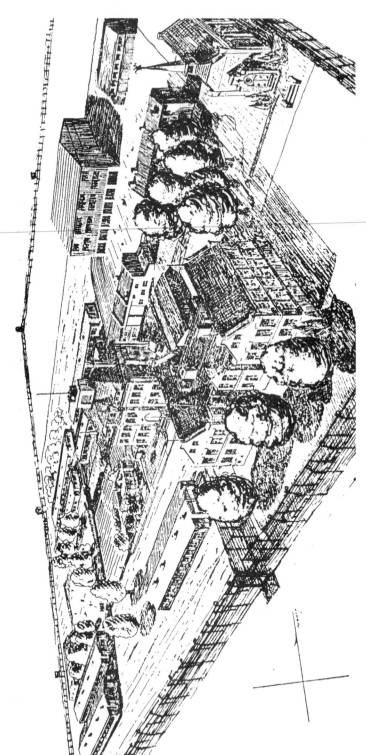

Oflag 64, the German prison camp for American ground force officers, is shown here in a sketch drawn by Lt. James Bickers for the camp paper. The barbed-wire fencing was left out of the original drawing on orders from the German commandant. Bickers added the barbed wire later for this rendition to show how it really looked. The camp was originally a 10-acre Polish boys' school, used at the start of the war to house British officers.

In addition, there were two long, brick barracks then in use, plus half a dozen more in an area marked off by a wire fence for use as the camp expanded. A small, attractive but badly run-down chapel, a greenhouse and a barn of some kind completed the facility. Not long before, the camp had been used to house British officer POWs. It all looked very strange and somber, with a few Americans now walking around as if they had somewhere to go.

I was greeted, given a very welcome Red Cross food parcel, and assigned to the big dormitory on the second floor of the White House, as the main building was called. My friend Larry Phelan and I were to share a double-deck bunk in the room with some 40 other "kriegies"—short for *Kriegsgefangeners* or prisoners of war. The room was furnished with six wash basins, a small indoor toilet and five very dim lights that were left on until "lights out" occurred every evening.

After settling in, I was carefully interviewed by the camp security officer, Lt. Col. James Alger, who explained that the Germans sometimes tried to sneak an English-speaking spy into the camp to uncover any escape plans. He wanted to make sure we newcomers were all really American Army officers. I remembered the ersatz Canadian from my days in solitary and agreed that the Germans were devious that way.

We walked around the camp and talked with the resident kriegies to see just how tough this internment was going to be. As prison camps go, it appeared that Oflag 64 had a lot going for it. No torture and no solitary confinement thus far had been reported. No officers were forced to really work. The wounded were pretty well taken care of in the camp hospital and another larger facility in the nearby town. Treatment had been fair up to now; the camp had been in business for American officers less than a year, with only about 200 now in residence, all of them taken in the Tunisian fiasco.

I soon discovered, however, that in addition to constant boredom, two overwhelming problems that made life difficult for everybody. You just could not get enough to eat, a problem that would get gradually worse as the war wore on. And during the bitter cold of winters in northern Poland there was no way to stay warm enough.

When I arrived in October 1943, Red Cross food parcels were distributed to each prisoner nearly every week. Supposed to be a food supplement only, the individual parcels contained enough nutrition for a man to subsist on for a week,

Kriegsgefangenen-Offz.-Lager 64
(Oflag 64)

Datum: **17.8.1944**

Ungültig als Legitimation für den öffentlichen Verkehr. **Ungültig**

Gültig NUR im Kriegsgefangenen-Lager.

Oflag 64

Der Kgf. hat diese Erkennungskarte und die Erkennungsmarke des Lagers stets bei sich zu führen. Bei Kontrolle sind beide vorzuzeigen. Verlust ist sofort zu melden.	The P. o. W. has always to carry with him this identification card and his tag. On control both have to be presented. The loss of the card or tag has to be reported immediately.

Name **Bickers jr. James F.**

Dienstgrad **Oberleutnant**

Erkennungs-Nr. **1472/IXA**

Fingerabdruck d. r. Z. F.

T/0357 8:4 WK

Photo of a typical identity card, issued by the Germans to all new prisoners of war early in World War II, including the prisoner's POW number and photograph. This one was issued to Lt. Bickers, one of the first arrivals from the U.S. military fiasco in North Africa.

things like a can of powdered milk, a bar of hard chocolate, some instant coffee, a tin of some kind of meat, even some cigarettes.

The German food ration for POWs, which was supposed to be equal to the ration provided to the German troops according to the Geneva Convention, had never been adequate. During that first week, I sampled what was being offered: a thin barley soup, some wizened turnips, and perhaps a shriveled-up carrot, plus about two inches of wartime black bread and sometimes old cabbage or potatoes. Each table of eight or ten officers at dinner would choose a trusted carver whose job it was to slice up the provided loaf of the German bread into exactly equal portions. The bread seemed to be mostly sawdust. The carving was done with extreme care with the carver always taking the last piece, so as to insure his accuracy. Many kriegies would take their portion back to the

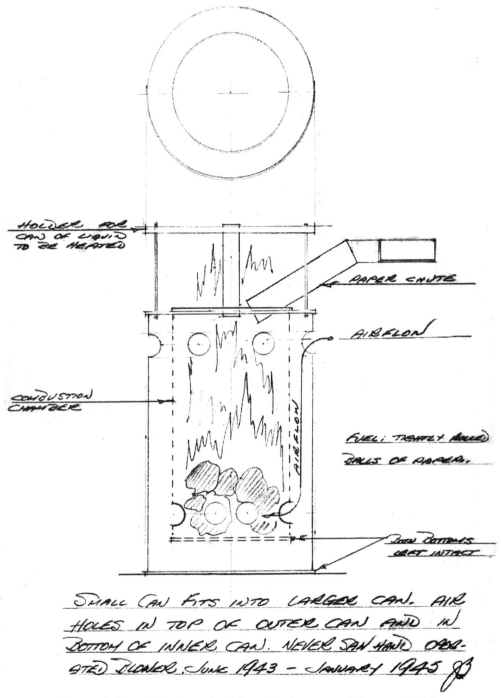

HOLDER FOR
CAN OF LIQUID
TO BE HEATED

PAPER CHUTE

AIRFLOW

COMBUSTION
CHAMBER

AIRFLOW

FUEL: TIGHTLY ROLLED
BALLS OF PAPER.

BOTH BOTTOMS
LEFT INTACT

SMALL CAN FITS INTO LARGER CAN. AIR
HOLES IN TOP OF OUTER CAN AND IN
BOTTOM OF INNER CAN. NEVER SAW HAND OPER-
ATED BLOWER. JUNE 1943 - JANUARY 1945

A diagram of the so-called "smokeless heaters" widely used in the camp made from used Red Cross powdered milk tins. Designed by an American engineer officer, they burned old German newspapers to heat water for Red Cross instant coffee.

barrack and slice the bread as thin as possible and toast it over what was known as a "smokeless heater," a camp specialty made from old Red Cross powdered milk tins. Heat was provided by burning pieces of German newspapers which were provided by the Reich's propaganda ministry.

This German food, such as it was, was brought in daily and prepared by half a dozen American enlisted POWs, who had volunteered for duty at Oflag 64, under the direction of our mess officer, then Lt. Col. Walter Oaks. The KP was not much of a job, except for peeling the few rotten potatoes. On one occasion, Col. Oaks looked the results of what they had done and said, "Now peel those peels." So they did. It seems there was a little bit of potato left on each peel and food was very scarce.

When I arrived in the fall, with fighting now going on in Italy, the weather in Poland was chilly but bearable. In a few weeks, though, the temperature indoors hovered around 40 degrees no matter what, and below freezing at night. The only warmth provided by the Germans came from old European porcelain stoves placed in each barrack and dormitory. Each morning we were given pressed peat bricks which we ignited and placed inside each stove. The bricks made the smooth tiles on the outside slightly warm, but never hot. "I always thought," one officer muttered later, "that it was the kriegies huddled around those stoves that kept them warm." At night, each man slept in all the clothes he owned and spread his GI overcoat atop the one thin blanket provided. This arrangement helped, I found, but not much.

What to do in the cold Polish evenings presented another problem. Most kriegies tended to huddle around the ceramic stoves for reading, bull sessions or some psychological warmth. Larry and I found an old deck of playing cards and soon established a nightly bridge session with another couple of bunk-mates, Lts. Howard Holder and George Durgin. We played under the dim overhead light with the simple expedient of playing with gloves on. The gloves didn't help our bridge any but it seemed to work.

Inside the camp, I found that things were run almost entirely by the ranking American officers. Discipline was tight. Everybody had to shave every day and abide by the rules set up by the senior American officer, known as the SAO, who at that time was Col. Thomas Drake. Drake was a no-nonsense officer who had served in World War I and whose regiment had been overrun in North Africa on Valentine's Day, 1943.

Some special friends at Oflag 64: front row (L to R)—Lts. George Durgin, Russ Ford, and Larry Phelan; back row—Unidentified officer and Lt. Lou Otterbien.

The story of how this ramrod-stiff American colonel first met with the camp's German commandant, *Oberst* Schneider, became a classic and went something like this: Col. Drake and an interpreter were called to the commandant's quarters for an initial conference. When they were seated, the German rose and began speaking in a loud "voice of command." The American colonel then rose up, beckoning to his interpreter, and started for the door. *Oberst* Schneider said *"Was ist los?"* Using his interpreter to emphasize his position of rank, Col. Drake said, "I am a colonel in the United States Army. One does not address an American colonel in that tone of voice. When you have learned to act and speak as an officer and a gentleman, I will return for the conference."

Schneider never again raised his voice in speaking to Drake. The senior American had established a control that turned out to be of great benefit to the rest of us for the nearly two years of sometimes tough captivity.

My other fellow kriegies were mostly young lieutenants or captains with a sprinkling of majors and light colonels to keep us in line. The average age was 27 years. Almost everyone was college-educated; many had advanced degrees. There were engineers, lawyers, doctors, journalists, artists, ranchers, musicians, even a former commandant of a Southern military academy. There were also a few West Pointers, but only a handful of professional soldiers otherwise. There were no blacks and no women in the camp. About half of us were married. Later on, all of the then 48 states were represented in our ranks, with 108 officers from New York, 58 from Pennsylvania, 74 from Texas, 2 each from Delaware, Montana, Rhode Island, Utah and Wyoming, plus 13 from Washington, D.C. and 3 from Hawaii. When I first arrived, the camp was small and I had a chance to meet almost everybody.

I soon fell into the normal, boring camp routine for the day, which started with the ringing of a loud bell sometime between 7:30 and 8 o'clock. Everybody would then tumble out for the first formation of the day. This was called *appell*, a Geman word with the accent strangely on the second syllable. During the two or three formations every day, we would all assemble on the camp parade ground to be counted by the Germans and often lectured by the German commandant, *Oberst* Schneider. This lecture involved his saying a few sentences in German, followed by a translation into much-shortened English by his interpreter, at which time the commandant would take one step to his left. A long speech could sometimes result in a 30-foot progression to the left. The counting

Group pictures were taken of the American prisoners wearing new Red Cross-supplied overcoats during the winter of 1943. Ice-skating became a popular sport of sorts that winter when the baseball diamond was flooded and frozen.

procedure was very methodical, often complicated by some kriegies moving about to confuse the counter. As winter came on, it grew very cold standing at *appell* for perhaps half an hour, so this practice was discouraged. Any prisoners who were late for the "fall in" call were forced to remain for another half an hour, so almost everyone was punctual. Another *appell* would be called in the afternoon, with an occasional third one thrown in by the Germans in an attempt to trap any prisoners who might be engaged in digging a tunnel. The Germans almost caught us a few times, but the tunnel diggers always managed to change and fall in just in time.

Appell ruled our lives in many ways; it was always inconvenient, whatever we were doing at the time. At one time, when I was editing the camp paper, I asked Dick Rossback (the train escapee who was later recaptured and sent onto Oflag 64) to do a humor column about it. Here is the little gem he produced:

OH HELL, THE BELL

The Bell
Oh hark how near, how loud and clear
You hear the clanging of the bell;
It chills your bones with mournful tones:
'Tis time now for appell.

The Chorus
Hurry, hurry, get your things,
Quick the moment that it rings.
Grab your cap; put on your coat;
Follow that compelling note.

Solo
Oh stay in check for just a sec,
Withhold your voice impending.
Please, please desist! You won't be missed;
I've got some toast I'm tending.
It's just begun ('twill soon be done)
A tasty tan to turn.
The marge is near with which to smear;
Come on you coals and burn.

The Bell

The echoes die, the kriegies fly,
No wonder to behold—
The tardy man must later plan
To shiver in the cold.

The Chorus

Hurry, Hurry, faster yet!
Throw away that cigarette.
Seconds tick, the clock won't wait—
Quicker, quicker, you'll be late.

Solo

My toast is spoiled, my coffee's boiled
Away, a sticky mess.
I curse the day, I cannot stay;
Oh weep for my distress.
My legs dig in, my lungs begin
To pound away within.
A final chase! I'm in my place,
And just in time: "Fall in!"

After morning *appell*, breakfast was a simple matter. It consisted of only hot water, plus whatever you had squirreled away. So everybody made his own, with Red Cross instant coffee, if he had any left over from his last parcel, and maybe a piece of toasted sour black bread hoarded from last night's so-called meal. Lunch consisted usually of a bowl of cabbage soup.

What to do for the rest of the day, between meals and *appells*, posed a problem. To stay sane, everyone needed a project and opportunities started to develop. A library of a few hundred old English novels, left over from when British officers were quartered there, was being expanded under the direction of Capt. Parrot. Volumes were sent in by the YMCA, the Red Cross and prisoners' families back home. Athletic equipment was starting to arrive, thanks to the YMCA. The "escape artists" were getting their tunnel plans under way. Volunteers were needed for several camp projects and many came forth.

All these options helped to take the prisoners' minds off their problems. Americans do not take kindly to captivity, however. No one ever expected to be captured. There we were, prisoners in enemy hands, locked in a camp completely isolated from the rest of the world and dependent for everything on the often ruthless and completely unpredictable Germans. Also, we were in the most escape-proof camp the Germans could devise. I found it more than a little traumatic, unsettling, and hard to get used to. I wondered naturally how most of my fellow American prisoners were coping. I found a few who had withdrawn into themselves, nearly all of them obsessed with taking the blame for the deaths of men under their command. Most of the others seemed to be coping very well despite the hardships of prison life, once they became involved in a project of some kind.

Aside from big escape projects, which involved everybody to some degree, the obvious answer to the question of staying sane was to get involved in a program where you might learn something. To meet this demand, an elaborate program of academic classes was being set up at this time by several officers with educational backgrounds under the direction of Capt. Hubert Eldridge, who had had 22 years of experience as a teacher and school superintendent. Designed as a college curriculum, it was known formally as Altburgund Academy (for the German name for Schubin) and, more informally, as the "Kriegy Kollege of Diabolical Knowledge."

As the weeks went on, this program became a great success. It offered 14 different courses, attended by almost everyone in camp. There were classes in German, Spanish, French, social science, physics, algebra, geometry, literature, speech and even journalism, which I taught on a once-a-week basis. There was also a surprisingly well-attended course, called Salesmanship, taught by Maj. Jerry Sage, the kriegy who held the record for the most number of successful escapes from various camps since his capture.

My class in newspapering had a star pupil in Lt. Frank Hancock, who was probably the youngest officer in camp. He had started to go to medical school before the war and intended to go back in order to become a rich and famous doctor, he said. He took to the craft of writing news like a duck to water and soon contributed mightily to the camp paper. After the war, Frank forgot about medical school and instead became a highly successful reporter and editor with a daily newspaper in Roanoke, Virginia. He enjoyed his writing career greatly but said later he never forgave me for steering him away from a doctor's life of luxury and ease.

The entertainment-starved prisoners very much enjoyed the plays put on from time to time in the Little Theater constructed by the Americans themselves. In addition to half a dozen Broadway-style plays, the theatrical group provided concerts, weekly humorous lectures, and special performances written by POWs. Note that the female roles were played by not-very-convincing male kriegies.

When the camp first opened, prisoners were paid a monthly salary based on their rank in accordance with the Geneva Convention. This *Kriegsgefangener gelt* was usable only within the camp, although virtually nothing was provided by the Germans to buy with it.

The other major project getting underway at this time to help keep American prisoners occupied and sane was a theatrical program put together by several talented officers with some theater and musical background. This project included a variety of plays, skits, concerts, reviews, lectures and camp celebrations. There was something going on at least once a week after the program got underway. Lt. Lou Otterbein, the camp handyman, actually built the "Little Theater" with lumber provided by the YMCA and the Germans. The International YMCA shipped in all sorts of theatrical equipment plus the scores of several Broadway-type shows. About 15 kriegies were involved in this project, most of them New Yorkers. Sparkplug of the group was Lt. Frank Maxwell. Others included Lts. Russ Ford, Bob Rankin, John Glendenning, Dick Van Sycle, Howard Holder, and Larry Phelan.

As Lt. Don Waful, one of the leaders of the theatrical group, described it later: "It was a rewarding task to select the plays to be presented, choosing the producers to cast and direct each one, picking men who would create skits and reviews, build the sets, develop the costumes and makeup, schedule rehearsal times and set up a calendar of opening nights."

Broadway shows were the most popular. The first hit was *Three Men on a Horse.* Another early one was *The Petrified Forest.* But the most ambitious of these supershows was *The Man Who Came to Dinner,* starring former actor Lt. John Hannan as Sheridan Whiteside. Musical performances were especially welcome. Lt. Bob Rankin, with his YMCA trumpet, put together a very professional "Big Band" concert featuring ballads, swing, and a trio of vocalists. From time to time later on, the band did a special musical news show, emphasizing the wartime hit songs and major news events of different eras.

At this early stage in 1943 and early 1944, the camp was operated by German regular army officers, who tended to follow army regulations and treat their American officer prisoners with a certain degree of respect. They did not always abide by the Geneva Convention. The food rations in particular were far below the quantity and quality of those provided for German troops. Pay for prisoners, required by the Convention, was honored briefly and only in theory. Punishment for escapees far exceeded that permitted by the Convention. Even so there were attempts at fair treatment. Some escorted walks were even permitted outside the camp. These walks could be made only by officers who agreed not to try escaping and were thus not very well attended.

Early on, when the Germans were still making a small effort to comply with Geneva, the American war prisoners were paid a token monthly salary in *Kriegsgefangener* script, which could be used only in the camp canteen. Unfortunately, there was little to buy there. The main items were three brands of German powder: *Zahnpuder* (tooth powder), *Fusspuder* (foot powder), and *Korperpuder* (body powder). They were all of the same consistency, and we doubted if they were different at all. For a brief time, the canteen also sold a foul brand of ersatz beer, a few strange French cigarettes called *Elegantes,* and a face cream, which we found made excellent shoe polish. The officer in charge was Lt. Col. Louis Gershenow. The canteen, which became a popular hang-out for bored kriegies, became known as Gershenow's Gaudy Gadget Shop. The walls were covered with funny cartoons by Lt. Jim Bickers, usually showing Germans as "goons" doing some outlandish thing.

Trading between kriegies soon proved to be a more practical way of acquiring anything, so this led to the formation of a "Schubin Merchandise Mart," set up by five enterprising young lieutenants, Ken Goddard, James MacArevey, Sid Thal, Ed Ward, and John Glendenning. The trading was based on a point system, so anyone with anything to trade would bring it in and get a specified number of points for it. With these points, he could "buy" whatever was available at the mart. Powdered milk, for example, was valued at 150 points. A 4-ounce can of coffee brought in 150 points. Cigarettes were in great demand; the point value varied with the supply on hand.

Activities on the mart were covered closely by *The Item,* our camp paper. One article was headed, "Milk Stocks Soar as Salmon Sags on Mart." It read: "Lt. Ed Spicher from Pleasant Gap, Pa., big margarine operator, last month broke all records for large trading operations at the Mart. His ticker tape record: 4,000 points across the board and 3,975 points withdrawn. 'My success lies in never trading on the margin,' said Ed modestly, munching a D-bar dividend. Heaviest Mart trading for the month was powdered milk, 15,300 points being deposited and 75 % withdrawn. Trading was steady in cigarettes, brisk in prunes, sluggish in cheese. With a steady increase in daily turnover, the monthly deposits totaled over 111,774 points and withdrawals 98,816."

Not long after I arrived, there was the strange case of young Lt. Bob Bonomi's "all expenses paid" trip to Berlin. This trip was in response to a German request for an American officer to volunteer to work on a German-run, English-language paper, called *The Overseas Kid,* aimed at American POWs. It sounded very phony to us, but Bob volunteered and got permission from Col. Drake to go to Berlin for an interview with some unnamed official of the Reich. Two German guards accompanied him on the train to Berlin, where he spent the first night in a building near the Brandenburg Gate, along with two Russian prisoners and one British corporal. The British non-com introduced one of the Russians as Stalin's son. He could have been; he didn't say. The next day Bonomi was escorted by a German soldier through the crowded Berlin subway to a mysterious garden and a large three-story building with a windowless wall and just steel-plated door. The door opened as they arrived and the escort was conducted away.

After an extended wait, seated on a straight chair near a very nervous blond German secretary, he was invited up to a two-rise entry into a rather large office. Two men were seated at a desk, one wearing a soldier's tunic with no emblems of any kind to indicate rank, service, or branch; the other was wearing a dark blue civilian suit with a white shirt and sincere dark tie. They shuffled papers and ignored Bob for a long time. Then the tunic-wearer came over to the American and said very plainly but quietly, *"Reichminister* Goebbels."

Bob saluted and Goebbels came around the desk and shook hands, then gestured for him to be seated. The German spoke in English, asking if the men in our camp had seen the initial issue of *The Overseas Kid.*

Bob tells what happened next:

"I said we had. He asked what the officers thought of it. I told him I thought they had enjoyed seeing it. He asked what part of the publication they liked the most. I said I believed they most enjoyed reading the German war communiques.

"At this reply, *Reichminister* Goebbels broke out with a smile of delight and success, seeming to actually swell with pride. As Minister of Propaganda, this daily communique was his baby. His chest expanded as he turned to his aide, then back to me. He asked, 'Why do they like the communiques?'

"'Because they show that Germany is losing the war,' I responded. Goebbels crumpled as if he had been punctured. He leaned his right hand on the desk and bent forward. His face twisted as he said, 'But I thought you wanted to help us.' My response was, 'I want to do the best I can to help those Americans who are your prisoners.'

"Goebbels said nothing, but was still leaning forward as he nodded to the tunic, who beckoned to me. I was summarily escorted out the door, then handed over to a guard who took me to an Italian Officer POW camp at Zehlendorf West. I have many times since realized that Goebbels could have consigned me to many places rather than returning me to Oflag 64. But that was all there was to it. There was no further interview. The two guards from Oflag 64 picked me up at 6 p.m. and we caught the midnight train back to Poland."

Later on, two other officers from Oflag 64 were ordered to leave the camp on another unusual mission, the case of the Katyn forest massacre. The German High Command had ordered two of our kriegies, Lt. Col. John Van Vliet and

Capt. Don Stewart along with two British officer POWs to go to the scene of the terrible slaughter of some 100,000 Polish army officers at Katyn forest. The Germans wanted to use the allied prisoners as witnesses to prove that the Russians, not the Germans, were responsible.

As the three kriegies watched, the Germans dug up more and more bodies and pointed out the Russian methodology used to kill them all, a single shot to the back of the head. The silent kriegies assumed at first that the Germans were guilty of the atrocity as they were of many others, but they became slowly convinced that it was the Russians after all. As Jack Van Vliet explained, "It was the fact that all of the Polish officers had been wearing new shoes that surprised and convinced us, not the elaborate show the Germans put on. As old prisoners ourselves, we knew that shoes wear out quickly in a prison camp, so that Polish officers had to have been murdered very soon after they were captured in 1939, when the Russians were controlling that half of Poland and long before the Germans took it over."

Our kriegies agreed among themselves that they would not report until after the war their conviction that the Russians must have been responsible for the massacre. So they said nothing upon their return to camp. After the war they wrote a full report to the Pentagon in 1945. That report, incidentally, disappeared mysteriously from Pentagon files and was later rewritten by Lt. Col. Van Vliet for a committee of Congress. Years later it was made public and eventually the Russians admitted their guilt.

Meanwhile, we remained at Oflag 64, faced with the prospect of awful boredom of years in a nearly escape-proof German prison camp in the middle of isolated Poland.

The Escape Artists

4 In the back of every American prisoner's mind at Oflag 64 was the matter of how to escape from this camp and somehow get out through Poland and across Russia or maybe the Baltic. Col. Drake's official Escape Committee had to approve all escape plans. The kriegies came up with all sorts of clever, unique and sometimes desperate plans for approval.

A tunnel under the barbed-wire fence was the obvious answer. That tunnel was always the main project, one that eventually involved almost everybody. Engineer officers in the camp devised an ingenious plan for a tunnel to start in a bathroom in one of the brick barracks and go deep underneath the fencing, surfacing in an unlikely place on the outside. We knew that the Germans had wires that led to underground microphones in the fence all around the camp. These microphones were believed to be sensitive to a depth of 30 feet. So the tunnel was designed to go down 40 feet. At this depth, the sandy Polish soil had a yellow tinge that made it impossible to spread on the gardens, so something over 56 tons of dirt were ultimately and precariously stored in empty Red Cross boxes placed in the shallow attics of all 14 barracks. On one occasion, the dirt-filled boxes did break through a ceiling but that damage was repaired before it was found by the Germans.

Unable to find the tunnel that they were certain was being dug, the Germans brought in a post-hole driller and sank 10-foot holes along the barbed-wire fence every 100 feet and placed explosives in them. These were exploded at random and thus caved in some of the tunnel. The explosions also cracked some of the windows in camp and caused tell-tale cracks to appear in the ceilings of some of the barracks where the dirt was stored overhead. The cracks were concealed cosmetically with dust and toothpaste, but this hardly calmed the kriegies who slept in the top bunks under them.

Finally, all the possible space available to store dirt in the barracks was filled. What to do with the stuff still being dug out of the growing tunnel every day? The solution lay in sprinkling it around the camp. So the clever tunnelers sewed sacks inside the trousers of some of the kriegies and filled them with dirt. As these prisoners walked around the 10-acre compound, they would pull a string releasing small quantities of dirt from time to time. That worked fine, getting rid of more tons of debris.

The tunnel also required shoring up, and that meant using wooden slats from our bunks. Everyone donated a slat, then another, then more until each man's thin mattress was held up by only three 6-inch-wide boards. That made sleeping very uncomfortable and sometimes hazardous, but the Germans never caught on.

When the tunnel was well along, months after I arrived, an almost identical tunnel was completed by the shot-down American and British flyers in the much larger German prison camp for captured airmen, Stalag Luft 3. This project became what was known to U.S. moviegoers later as *The Great Escape*. The tunnel worked, but unfortunately it was also a great disaster. That tunnel turned out to be just a little short. The escaping prisoners emerged within sight of one German guard. Of the 78 who emerged, only three got fully away. The rest were ultimately recaptured and some of them shot immediately. When Hitler heard of the escapes, he was furious and ordered 50 of the remaining escapees who were in German hands all to be shot. Thus, 50 of the American and British escapees were deliberately murdered by the Gestapo. This misfortune also spelled the end of our tunnel project on orders from Washington, I believe. Our tunnel remained, however, and was never found by the Germans. It was used successfully later on as a hiding place by a number of kriegies when the camp was evacuated and the prisoners marched back to Germany, so all that effort was not wasted.

Other individual escape attempts were made before and after the tunnel project. One of the most ingenious, which almost worked, was tried by five Americans who staged a fake drunken party. They made a great deal of noise one night for the purpose of getting thrown into the German camp jail, which happed to be outside the barbed wire and used chiefly to deal with German soldiers who misbehaved. Once in the jail, they would use a hacksaw blade adhesive-taped to the bottom of Lt. Dick Secor's foot to break out and take off for Sweden.

The booze was brewed from raisins by our clever cooks and was judged to be completely harmless but convincing nonetheless. My friend, Lt. "Tex" Chappell, had the loudest voice and quickly convinced the Germans that the after-hours party was getting out of hand and must be stopped. Several German interpreters tried to convince the rowdy bunch to calm down and return to their barracks, as they might be shot. They refused, of course. Then the Germans called on the Senior American Officer who, naturally, was part of the act. He said, "Nothing doing, They're rowdy drunks and deserve to be punished." So finally, twelve big guards arrived and escorted the five kriegies out the gate and into the German jail, just as planned. *Oberst* Schneider ordered the Americans to spend two weeks in solitary confinement for disobedient drunken behavior. He specifically chewed out Lt. Col. Van Vliet, one of the "drunks," as a senior officer for setting a bad example for his juniors.

Sure enough, the homemade "keys" worked for all but Jack Van Vliet's cell, so on the last day at dusk, four of the clever kriegies escaped from the jail and worked their way for several blocks toward freedom. Unluckily, they were then sighted by an off-duty guard and quickly recaptured. The German commandant realized he had been hoodwinked, but the Reich at that time was still abiding by the Geneva Convention provision that POW escapees could not be punished, much less shot.

At about the same time, a fellow-kriegy named Lt. Nelson Tacy and I started to work on a stand-by plan for escaping in case the right opportunity arose. Nelson was a scholarly New Englander who was married to a German-American girl back home and said he knew how the Teutonic mind worked. He had located an old Polish sled in the basement of the White House and figured that if we could disguise ourselves as one arrogant German soldier and one beaten-down Polish worker dragging the sled, we might get away without anybody stopping us. We began to work on our plan by finding some props that would work as a disguise. I located some material that I shaped into something that might look like a German helmet, if the light were very dim, and shaped a stick to vaguely resemble a German rifle. Nelson practiced pulling the sled and looking subservient while wearing a Polish-looking hat. That stage was as far as we got at the time, but this unlikely plan would come in exceedingly handy later, when conditions changed.

Most escape plans were worked up by small groups of two to five prisoners, then submitted to the camp security committee which had to approve them before they could be attempted. In only one case was a plan approved for a single kriegy and it almost worked. An enlisted man who had volunteered for duty at Oflag 64 managed to hide in the back of a German truck which came in and out of the camp often with supplies of food and coal. The truck pulled out through the main gate with the sergeant inside, but for some reason, instead of driving on as usual, it merely crossed the road and parked in front of the German guardhouse. Eventually one of the ever-present police dogs which the guards always kept around the camp happened to catch the unlucky sergeant's scent, commenced barking, and disclosed his hiding place.

A typical escape plan, however, involved months of planning, much preparation and elaborate technical assistance on the part of several people. Take, for example, the plan worked out by my early roommates, Lts. Howard Holder and George Durgin. It went something like this:

To begin with, they needed to accumulate many things—maps, directions, food, canteens, and a compass. In addition, they needed to be in excellent physical condition for the expected long hike out of Poland. This they set out to do and acquire during the winter months of 1943. Where to go after they got out was the first problem and they picked the closest haven possible, the port of Danzig. That was about 100 miles away, which they figured they could walk within 10 or 12 days. Then they would hop a Swedish freighter, stow away to Sweden, somehow reach an American consulate there and eventually fly home. That would be a big gamble, but they figured it could work with enough preparation and a bit of luck.

How to get through the awesome double barbed wire fencing and out of the camp was another major problem, this being a supposedly escape-proof prison camp with all the latest German electronic gadgetry in place. They carefully examined the entire fencing around the 10-acre camp and concluded there was no way to get over the double fifteen-foot fence of barbed wire. So they logically decided that the best way to get out of the compound was the same way they got in—through the main gate. It was a huge double gate, about eight feet wide, or about the same distance as the two barbed wire fences were apart. Inside of the gate was the same collar of rolled-up barbed wire that extended between the double fence around the camp. But there was one possibility: the gates were constructed with lattice-work metal beams which looked to be exceedingly easy to climb.

The only question remaining was how to climb over the gates without being seen and shot. A daytime attempt was impossible, of course. But maybe at night during a heavy rainstorm, when the guards were taking shelter and not watching the gate. So they carefully checked the layout. The closest sentry box was within thirty yards of the gate. The only tower from which the guards could get a clear shot at the main gate was two hundred yards away at the other end of the compound. In the rain, they thought this guard would not be able to see the gate clearly, and verified this by checking the view from there during the next foggy period.

So on this basis, Holder and Durgin got a go-ahead from the security committee, on the understanding that the escape attempt would only be made after midnight during a heavy rainstorm that summer. Help was provided in the form of maps, fake identity papers, and much good advice. They were told they would need to take enough food and water for 14 days. in order to not be dependent on the Poles during their hike to Danzig. The doctors in the camp had worked out a formula for combining foods with the highest vitamin content into a compact and edible cake which would provide the maximum food value and high caloric content with the minimum amount of weight and space. Durgin, who was a skilled engineer, designed a practical knapsack eighteen inches long, fifteen inches wide and four or five inches deep, which would hold exactly the amount of food and water they needed to carry. Then they began to swap their own cigarette rations for the priceless food that other kriegies had squirreled away, and slowly assembled their escape rations. At one point a German security guard came upon them while they were busily engrossed in rolling C biscuits into crumbs to be added to a pile of other such ingredients. But he merely smiled and asked "Kuchen machen?" (Are you making cake?) They replied "Ja Ja" and added that it was for their eight-man mess table. The German nodded and went away, fortunately.

Getting into shape for the walk of one hundred miles was also a real job. Every day they did as much strenuous exercise as they could, walking or running on the cinder exercise walkway in the camp. They always staggered their exercise hours so that the guards would not become too suspicious of their sudden regular activity. They started out walking three or four miles a day, and gradually increased the mileage to eight or ten. By April they were in relatively fine shape and didn't doubt that they could do the distance to Danzig with no trouble at all.

Now they assembled all of their escape rations and devices into the carefully-designed knapsacks, made from some gunny sacking and an old army fatigue jacket and sewed together meticulously by hand. They wanted these important knapsacks to look as inconspicuous as possible, so they decided to dye them a nondescript brownish color like those on the backs of many of the Polish people walking by the camp. This brought up the question of what to use for dye. They experimented with different agents on small pieces of cloth to get an idea of how each prospective dye would look. They tried lead from some indelible pencils they found in a former classroom, but this was too purple. Next they tried potassium permangamate which was used by the hospital as a treatment for athlete's foot, but this turned the material a bright purple. Finally Durgin hit on the idea of using ersatz coffee which was then a part of the German food ration, and their cloth came out a beautiful brown color that was similar to that of the local knapsacks.

For shoulder straps they used a pair of British suspenders, about one and a half inches wide, which they had acquired in a previous camp before reaching Oflag 64. For a canteen, they used an old cookie tin from a British Red Cross box issued at the same camp, with a cork which had been brought into this camp to use, when burnt, for blackening faces in a camp minstral show. More importantly, they needed a compass and fortunately they had a crude one which they had slipped out of the British camp at Rotenburg. It was a rough, homemade job, but it worked fine, being a simple piece of magnetized metal balanced on a small mount.

By the end of April, four months after they began to plan their escape, they were ready to go. Holder and Durgin had marked out their planned trip every inch of the way, and knew their route by heart without a map. Their food for 14 days was carefully packed away in their brown knapsacks, and they were in good physical condition. All that was needed now was a good night with plenty of rain. They started waiting for a rainy night, taking turns each night staying up until dawn in order not to miss a single chance. Even when it didn't look cloudy, one of them stayed up all night, just in case. Unfortunately the weather in northern Poland refused to cooperate and night after night there was no heavy rain.

Then came one night that was overcast and windy. It seemed to be about ready to rain hard, so they were both up and fully dressed when the main gate creaked open and three German guards came in for their regular nightly check of the barracks. The escapees were standing by Holder's bunk debating whether the guards had come into the White House when they suddenly saw a flash of light in the adjoining room. The guards were coming straight for the door to their room and there the two kriegies were standing by their bunk fully dressed. While the inspection occurred every night at the same time, it covered a different barrack each time, so the guards were not expected that night at the White House. There was no time to stop and think. They each jumped into their bunks, fully clothed, shoes and all. But due to their methodical nature, the guards came in and, ignoring the noise from bouncing beds, began their flashlight check at the other side of the room, going up and down each aisle to see if all kriegies were accounted for. All of them were, by the time blankets were pulled up over the potential escapees and gentle snores were sounding.

In May, much to their disgust, the doctors ruled that Durgin could not go out on the escape, due to a flare up of eczema on his hands that had been bothering him for some time. So they picked another well-qualified prisoner, Lt. Duane "Andy" Johnson from South Stanton, Iowa, to take his place. Andy was already in good shape, had been exercising regularly, and was very anxious to get out of Oflag 64. So George handed him his ready knapsack and reluctantly moved into the hospital.

Finally in June it looked like a heavy rain was about to fall one night, so Holder and Johnson were both up and dressed ready again to take advantage of their chance if it presented itself. At about midnight, a light shower started and they went downstairs to the Mess Hall where there was a window from which they could lower themselves to the ground. This was about fifteen feet below, but there was an old iron railing within reach of the window from which they might slide down. All the doors in every barrack were locked at night so this was the only way to get out. Holder went first and they were soon on the ground outside of the building. It wasn't raining very hard by this time, but they decided to try it anyway. They had alerted another kriegy, Lt. Bob Aschim, to signal them from the window when the German guard near the gate had gone into his little sentry box to get out of the rain, and he did so. So they crawled across to the big inner gate and started to climb up it when a hush fell over the camp. The covering rain had stopped and the two escapees were climbing with no cover at all.

As "Boomer" Holder tells what happened next: "We dropped down and stretched out flat on the ground. Then we heard the guard come out of his sentry box and commence walking his post again, not over a hundred feet from where we lay. We were in a tight spot and we knew it. We had to work fast because the guard could spot us at any time. We started back toward the White House. After crossing the open space, we reached the side of the building, clambered somehow back up the side of the wall and back through the window into the safety of the mess hall. We were covered with mud, but at least we had no bullet holes. We had not been discovered, although were extremely vulnerable. We waited up until dawn, but there was no more rain. We were disappointed once again."

Although they continued to stay up night after night, no occasion to escape presented itself until it was too late—three days after a no-escape order was given to everyone in the camp by the SAO. This occurred after the fifty escapees from Stalag Luft 3 were recaptured and murdered on Hitler's orders. Col. Drake reasoned that the risk was too great to permit any more escape attempts to be made this late in the war.

Three days after this order from our SAO was issued, there was a big thunder and lightning storm, during which, Holder says, "we could have walked out of the camp standing straight up. It was very frustrating."

Meanwhile, however, another clever escape attempt had been made that summer to get through the barbed wire fence in broad daylight, this one with a little more success. The plan was cooked up by Lts. Roy Chappell, Frank Aten and Archie Higgins, who had carefully scouted the fencing all around the camp and discovered one area where foliage was growing just inside the inner wire so that it almost hid that small sector from the view of the nearest guard towered on the east side. They waited for a few weeks for the weedy bush to grow higher and got permission from the escape committee to try a daylight breakthrough, with the help of a set of wire cutters obtained from a Polish workman by bartering some kriegy coffee and cigarettes. This spot was directly opposite the west side entrance to the German commandant's home outside the camp.

The trio of lieutenants drew straws to determine who would have the privilege of using the pliers first, and Chappell drew the short straw. The timing agreed to was about an hour and a half before the evening *appell*. While Aten and Higgins watched from nearby, "Tex" Chappell slipped under the trip wire that had been placed across a sand strip before the fence and cut completely through the wire enclosure. He crawled through and rose up outside of the fence, then walked as casually as possible down the front walk of the *Komandateur*, turned to the left on the street and proceeded east along the stone wall enclosing the adjacent cemetery, where he waited for his companions while being screened by a large tombstone.

Higgins and Aten followed promptly behind, but just before Aten reached the cemetery entrance an off-duty German guard happened to see him from the front of the nearby German barracks. He gave an immediate alarm as the escaped prisoners crouched behind the tombstones and hoped to avoid the omnipresent German guard dogs and well-armed soldiers. But the jig was up; the three were quickly found and recaptured. Their punishment for making the first successful escape from Oflag 64 was thirty days of solitary confinement on bread and water in the German jail across from the prison camp. The Nazi policy of murdering escaped and recaptured prisoners would come later.

Prisoners Who Made
a Difference

5 The camp was especially fortunate in having a number of talented and energetic Americans, who were willing and able to take on roles that made a big difference in the lives of the rest of us. One was a modest, cheerful young lieutenant named John L. Creech, who happened to have a brand-new college degree in floriculture. John knew that the biggest problem facing all of us was the serious shortage of food. He asked for, and got permission to use, an old greenhouse plus two-and-a-half acres of land in the compound to grow food for the American prisoners. Why not, the Germans said? So he and several other kriegies, with a lot of back-breaking effort, spaded up the plot. Then he created "flats" for the greenhouse with used Red Cross cartons. With seeds he somehow received from home, John started some 6,000 tomato plants and filled three cold frames with beet and lettuce seeds. The Germans were popeyed at his tomatoes, Marglobe, Bonny Best, and giant Ponderosa. Leeks then became a staple in the kriegy diet. John had apparently gotten several thousand leek and onion plants from some source in town. Once word of this achievement got out, more seeds poured in from other sources, the American Red Cross, the Royal Horticultural Society, the French and the Dutch.

Even this additional food remained too small to stop our weight-loss. John's crops, however, made a substantial difference in balancing our diet as the camp's American population increased rapidly. At one point, the Gestapo grew suspicious of all that digging and

Prisoners pose before the old greenhouse that was taken over by Lt. John Creech to grow desperately needed food from seeds provided by the Red Cross.

came into camp to dig up part of the plot where kriegies were spending so much time. John appreciated the help as we would not have to plow that section ourselves. After the war, Lt. Creech became Dr. Creech, with an international reputation as Director of the National Arboretum in Washington, D.C. and for developing new plants of many kinds.

Another indispensable kriegy at Oflag 64 was young Lt. Jim Shoaf. He was a quiet electronic genius who kept us in touch with the outside world by creating a workable secret radio out of the unlikely stuff available in a remote prison camp, plus one smuggled-in vacuum tube. While at a British officers' camp at Rothenberg, Jim learned how a radio could be built. With the help of a Pentode (five-element) tube sealed in a biscuit tin, which the British officers gave him, he set out to build ours. So at Oflag 64, the American prisoners immediately started collecting old cigarette packs to make a foil electrode and wax paper from Red Cross parcels to make a thin homogeneous insulator. The necessary "resonant-coil" wire was obtained from an abandoned camp speaker, with a field-coil type magnet found in the White House.

Lt. Shoaf insisted that all this plan was simple. In any event, the first crystal set he built at Oflag 64 was made from these elements and worked quite well on its first trial. Then he went on to collect other needed items with which to make a "one-tube" set. This one became "The Bird," installed in the attic of the White House and tuned into the British Broadcasting Corporation (BBC) newscast from London. Every day at about 2 p.m., the news was received over "The Bird," and taken down verbatim by Lt. Frank Maxwell, who knew shorthand. This went on, undetected by the Germans, for two years until the camp was evacuated. Then "The Bird" was carried along by the marching kriegies to keep them up to date on the long march back to Germany. Jim operated it then in a series of haylofts, manure piles, pigpens and cellars.

At the camp, the news was read to four or five kriegy newscasters every afternoon. Then it would be read by them that evening after lights-out to men in their own barracks. The White House broadcaster was my bridge-playing friend, Howard Holder, a former radio newsman. He was always called "Boomer" because of his fine, strong voice, which he used often. Boomer also wrote a column for the camp paper. After the war, he returned to radio broadcasting and eventually owned and operated three radio stations in Athens, Georgia.

News from Jim's radio called for a special performance on D-Day of the Normandy invasion. Early that morning, the four broadcasters were called in and tipped off that the invasion had begun and where the landing hit. Thus, the news spread rapidly around the camp and the American prisoners knew about it before the Germans got the word from their brief radio announcement several hours later. As soon as the Germans got the word, our *Daily Bulletin* news sheet, which I was editing, came out with a special edition. The big headline read: "INVASION'" and the story covered as many details as the German radio divulged.

By an almost unbelievable coincidence, the camp had planned a big celebration on that same day for the first anniversary of American kriegies in Oflag 64, where they had arrived a year before. This celebration consisted of sports

A special edition of *The Daily Bulletin* was posted as soon as the German radio acknowledged that the Normandy invasion was underway. The Americans actually knew about the landing early that morning from a BBC broadcast picked up on their secret radio. Details about the size and location of the invasion were not provided by the Germans until days later.

tournaments of all kinds, plus an all-day show put on by the theater group. At the end of the big performance that night, the actors spread across the stage, each carrying a large letter which spelled out "LETS GO IKE." The Germans never believed that our celebration that day was a coincidence and assumed that we knew the date of the D-Day invasion well in advance.

A third hero of Oflag 64 was a clever, conscientious lieutenant named Don Lussenden. In need of a project, Don started the camp bookbindery. He became involved when the camp librarian sent out a call for somebody who could repair books for the library. Our library then contained some 250 well-worn volumes, which the preceding group of English officers had left behind. They were soon supplemented by American titles from the International YMCA and Red Cross. All of these books, old and new, had been machine-bound and were never intended for nonstop reading and handling. The glue and stitching soon broke down, allowing sections of the book to fall apart and the covers to come off. When the new and extremely popular American books began to break down after 10 or 20 readings, the call went out for a bookbinder.

Don, who had no experience in this field but had learned a bit from a Boy Scout merit badge project, came to the rescue. As he tells it, the library staff had the foresight to order bookbinding supplies at the same time that they asked the YMCA for new books from America. So Don started with a good supply of thread, needles, paper, artificial leather, and glue. And he said he had "plenty of beat-up books to start with."

Thus, the "Gnome Bookbindery" was born. Don explains: "In the attic of the White House there were a few storage areas. I selected a suitable space with a skylight roughly one foot square and a single light bulb hanging from a twisted cable. Using cardboard from old Red Cross food parcels, the walls and rafters were made reasonably weather-worthy. In addition, the cardboard was covered with white paper from our bookbinding supplies which reflected such light that was received from the single light bulb and skylight. The German staff provided a small wood-burning stove that took the chill off and kept the glue pot warm. The tools furnished by the YMCA included two knives, a shoemaker's hammer and a large wooden clamp made of two hardwood 3-inch-by-3-inch bars with a 1-inch wooden screw at each end. I must admit that our rebound books were not pleasing to the eye, but they were serviceable.

"After a few months of operation," Don went on, "we had a visit from a German guard, one Willi Kricks, who had lived in Schubin prior to 1939 and owned and operated a printing shop and bookbindery here. Willi was an *Auslander Deutscher*, and when the German Army occupied Poland, he suddenly became a German soldier. Handicapped with a crippled leg, he was attached to the local grenadier group and, of course, did the printing for the area military units. Later, in 1943, he also printed *The Oflag Item*, our camp newspaper.

"Naturally, Willi was interested in seeing his only competition in Schubin, so he came to visit us. He quickly found out that I was not an experienced bookbinder and asked if I would like to go downtown to his bookbindery and learn the trade from his employees. Formal arrangements were made, and the two of us were allowed to go each day for two weeks and work with four Polish workers in his bookbindery. It was a fine learning experience.

"Willi became a frequent visitor to the 'Gnome Bookbindery' and never left without a small present. I received permission from our SAO to barter with Willi to obtain needed supplies and services. We very early ran out of glue and heavy thread. For cigarettes, Willi kept us in supply of both. He also took our cutter blade to Danzig for sharpening when required. After our training session, he showed us a big surprise. It seems that there was a large book press and book trimmer hidden away in the building that housed the camp tailor shop. So we got it. This equipment took 10 kriegies to lift and carry down to the ground floor and again up to the third floor of the White House where our bookbindery was located. The new piece of equipment gave our work a professional appearance."

Frequently, Don reports, Col. Drake and his staff gave the Gnome bookbinders material to secret into their books to provide evidence in future war crime investigations of the German treatment of their prisoners of war. Before starting on such an evidence-hiding operation, Don would inform our security office that they would be working on the special bindings at a given time, so that a lookout could be posted to warn of any German guards entering the third-floor area. Had they been caught red-handed in the act, it would have been considered by the Nazi regime in the same category as spying. We found out later how serious that could be when several kriegies were tried and sentenced to be shot for less serious crimes.

The evidence to be hidden, he explained, "was carefully hand-printed on onionskin paper approximately 4 inches by 6 inches in size. Books then were selected by subject to later be matched with, and assigned to, an officer who would logically own such a book, e.g., an engineering manual for a mechanical engineer, a foreign language text for someone studying that language. After selection of the book was made, we would rebind it using the original cardboards. We slowly and carefully split the edges of the front and back cardboard covers into two thin sheets apiece. Then we outlined a space on the inside surfaces of the split boards to accommodate the onionskin evidence. After inserting the thin

Here are some of the top-ranking officers in the camp: (L to R) Lt. Col. John Waters (General Patton's capable son-in-law), Col. John L. Goode (the Senior American Officer at the time), a Red Cross representative, Lt. Col. Shaefer (later tried in a German court and ordered to be shot, but survived when the camp was evacuated), and Lt. Col. Millette.

paper, a colorless glue was used to seal the halves back into a cover board and then sanded to remove any evidence of the insert. The boards were assembled into the split, then assembled into a normal cover and attached to the newly bound book."

Needless to say, every kriegy benefited from Don's long volunteer work with the much-used books in the camp library, as did the war crime investigators later on.

The much-needed camp tailor shop, which mended and altered some 2,000 pairs of trousers and as many shirts over a two-and-a-half-year period, using three American sewing machines and one iron, was operated by Lt. Verris Hubbel and three aides, Lts. Donald Rockwell, Delbert Dorman, and Selwyn Goodman. The tailor shop also made costumes for the theatrical productions, including false breasts and hip pads for the female impersonators. They even made a ballet costume for use in *You Can't Take It With You.*

Then there was a camp pressing service, run by Capts. Warren Walters and Dalton Medlen. They pressed an average of 20 pairs of pants a day and reported handling some 5,000 pairs in all.

Kriegy shoes needed repairing too. From 10 to 15 pairs of badly worn Army shoes were made usable every day by the camp cobbler shop operated by Lt. Ormond Roberts and assisted by Lts. Art Bryant and Henry Desmond. All of this was performed with the help of an antiquated German sanding and buffing machine and an old Polish leather sewing machine.

To keep prisoners looking presentable if not happy, there was also a camp barber shop, operated by Lt. John Monks with five enlisted volunteers brought in as barbers. This crew handled an average of 350 customers a week. Each barber handled 15 haircuts a day, and each kriegy was eligible for one haircut every 21 days. They were not always professional, mind you, but not crewcuts either.

With food the center of every prisoner's attention, the camp kitchen was carefully operated by American officers, Lt. Col. William Martz and Lt. Col. Oaks, assisted by Capt. George Lucey, Capt. Allan White, Lts. Robert Aschim and Leo Farber. The ration officer was Capt. Joe Emerson. The camp cooks were all enlisted men: Sgt. D. C. Olson, who was a CCC cook before joining the Army, Sgt. M. D. Massey, Pfc. J. Patton and Pfc. L. A. Annunziata, who was a master baker in Brooklyn, New York. As the camp population expanded, this crew wound up preparing some 650 liters of soup, 1,056 pounds of potatoes, and 1,000 pounds of cabbage or turnips each day.

The senior officers at Oflag 64 were not idle either. Col. Drake was a busy, full-time camp commander, repatriated a few months after I arrived for medical reasons. He was succeeded ably by Col. Paul R. Goode as SAO. The staff, which ran the camp along strictly U.S. Army lines, included Col. George Millett as Executive Officer, Lt. Col. Max Gooler as assistant Executive Officer, and Col. F. W. Drury as Inspector General. Maj. Kermit Hansen served as S-1, Lt. Col. James Alger as S-2, Lt. Col. John Waters as S-3, Lt. Col. Louis Gershenow as S-4, and Capt. Floyd Burgeson as Chief Medical Officer.

An Unusual Newspaper

6 Shortly after I arrived in camp, I found my own project for forgetting about hunger pangs and staving off boredom. Another, older kriegy, Capt. George Juskalian, and I decided to start a camp newspaper to be turned out monthly, if possible. I laid out a dummy much like the college paper I had once edited and we got together a staff of 10 others with some journalistic experience.

To our great surprise, the Germans agreed not only to let have it but also to have it printed professionally. Thus, Oflag 64 became the only prison camp in the history of the world to have its own printed newspaper. No one yet knows why the Germans permitted this in view of their sorry record in other matters. But they did and *The Oflag Item* was published every month thereafter. It was printed by Willi Kricks, the same German guard who was operating a printing shop in nearby Schubin and who assisted Don Lussenden in setting up the camp bookbindery. With a staff of four Polish printers, Willi did a good job of it too after all the language typos were corrected.

So *The Item* started with its November 1943 issue as a 4-to-8-page monthly, designed to tell what was going on and maybe help morale in the camp a bit. It was informative, often funny, and with heavy emphasis on news from home, theatrical productions held and planned in camp, sports events, and upcoming camp projects. The paper was censored, of course, and each issue had to be marked

The Oflag 64 Item

All the News That's Been Geprüft

"Get Wise — ITEM-ize"

Largest Circulation Inside the Wire

No. 1   Altburgund, Germany — November, 1943   Price: 50 Pfg.

"Brother Orchid," Zippy 3-Acter, Hi-lites Thanksgiving

The first modern American three-act play to be presented at Oflag 64 will usher in the Thanksgiving holiday with a belly full of laughs in place of turkey.

"Brother Orchid" by Leo Brady is the name of the show.

Frank Maxwell hustles to perform the double duties of director and leading man, portraying Little John Sarto, big time gangster recently of Alcatraz.

Little John descends unceremoniously into the cloistered life of a monastery, where the pious Little Brothers of the Flowers, enacted by Lts. Casner, Sharpe, Hubbell and Bickers take up a tug of war against mobsters and racketeers for the soul of their new brother. Lts. Gever, Lobb, Hessler, Scherman and Koch provide worthy opposition as the gang element.

The show is tentatively scheduled to run November 25, 26, 27 inclusive.

Five Officers Receive Silver Star Awards

Silver Star awards will decorate the blouses of five more officers here, recent mail from the States reports. Post-capture citations have been made to Capt. Maynard Files and Lts. Milton Jellison, Herbert Johnson, John Creech and Anthony Cipriani.

These officers earned the "Gallantry in Action" award during the fight in which they were taken prisoners.

Capt. Files received his first Silver Star for gallantry during the landing operations at Oran. He won the Oak Leaf Cluster to the Silver Star for an attack at El Guettar, Tunisia, March 29, 1943, in which his company was in assault.

Lt. Jellison succesfully evacuated the major portion of two platoons from an encircled position at Kasserine Pass, Tunisia, on February 19, 1943.

Lt. Creech was on a mission ten miles beyond his own lines observing enemy movements. He was captured in the El Guettar area March 24, 1943.

For leading an assault platoon in an attack at El Guettar on March 28, 1943, the Silver Star was awarded to Lt. Cipriani.

Lt. Johnson was captured near Ousseltia, Tunisia, while leading a support party to aid a company which was being cut off.

Newest Arrivals Represent Twenty States, Mostly Texas

OFLAG CALENDAR

Nov.	Event	Time
3 —	"Wednesday at 7 : 15"	7 : 15 p
4,5 —	German Silent Films	7 : 00 p
6 —	Quiz Program : 20 VS 21	7 : 00 p
8 —	Lecture, Larry Allen	7 : 00 p
11,12	Bingo	7 : 00 p
13 —	Quiz Program : 22 VS.23	7 : 00 p
15 —	Lecture, Capt. Wilcox, "Law"	7 : 00 p
16 —	Book Review	7 : 00 p
17 —	"Wednesdays at 7 :15"	7 : 15 p
18,19	Minstel Show-Ford	7 : 00 p
20 —	Quiz Program : 24 VS.25	7 : 00 p
22 —	Travel Talk, Col. Alger	7 : 00 p
24 —	"Wednesdays at 7 : 15"	7 : 15 p
25 —	Thanksgiving	
25,26,27 —	"Brother Orchid", Maxwell	7 : 00 p
	Sundays — Catholic services	9 : 30 a
	General church services	10 : 30 a

Prem to Pinch-Hit For Turkey

All-American chow in large quantities will overload the Oflag tables on Thanksgiving, according to Lt. Col. W. M. Oakes, mess officer.

No, it isn't turkey, but the menu still looks mighty good. Look:

Breakfast: American Oatmeal.
Dinner: Meat and Vegetable hash à la Oakes.
Supper: Prem, mashed potatoes, peas, carrots — and may be dessert, depending on what shows up.

Minstrel Due Nov. 18—19

Blackface will take the spotlight when Russ (Al Jolson) Ford brings his twenty-odd minstrels to the footlights of The Little Theatre on November 18—19.

Howard Holder plays the dual role of scriptwriter and interlocuter.

End men: Messrs. Thal, Fabian, Waful and Cipriani.

Scharpe, Marlowe, Willis and Fabian, supply special numbers.

Lt. Straight Awarded DSC

For continuing a counterattack after his commanding officer had been put out of action, Lt. Fay Straight has been awarded the Distinguished Service Cross, it was learned this week.

During the course of the battle, Lt. Straight and his men were caught under heavy fire. Straight was able to evacuate most of his command but was unable to escape himself.

He was captured near Tebourba, Tunisia on December 6, 1942.

72 New Kriegies Report Here In October

The Oflag's Welcome Mat took a helluva beating last month when 72 new officers trudged through the gate.

Most of these are officers of a Texas regiment now fighting in Italy. Others include officers captured in Tunisia, an airborne battalion commander captured near Naples, an Associated Press correspondent with the British Royal Navy and a Catholic chaplain.

Lt. Col. Doyle Yardley was the first of the new comers, arriving here October 1. A paratrooper, he was captured before day break on September 15, having jumped at midnight with his battalion and landed near a panzer division command post.

On October 7, Capts. Newton Lantron and Joe Emerson, Lt. Dalton Medlen and W/O Roger Cannon, all of Texas, Lts. Theodore Pawloski and Steve Barcovic of Pennsylvania, and Lt. Wilbert Davis of Illinois arrived. They were captured near Naples.

They were followed on October 16 by Lt. P. D. Lumpra.

Thirty officers arrived on October 19, including the new chaplain, Lt. S. Brach of New Jersey, and three doctors, Capts. Wyson and Mackee of Ohio and Capt. T. E. Corcoran of Iowa.

With this group came AP correspondent and Pulitzer prize winner Larry Allen of West Virginia. Allen, in his three years as writer with the British Mediterranean fleet, had, up to the time of his capture, seen every naval operation in that sea and had been five times torpedoed, three times sunk.

Most of the officers in the October 19 group had been captured in Tunisia. The group included:

Capts. W. Walters, Ark., Yarock, Mass, and Hughes, Mass., Lts. Straight, W. Va., Higgins, Ia., Jones, Pa., McLaughlin, N.Y., Weigand,Ohio, La Chance, Ala., Fitton, Ark., Hirt, Ill., Matton, Okla., Carnes, Ind., Denman, Ala., Feldman, Mass., Victor, Ill., Frazee, Ohio, Long, Va., Johnson, Pa., Holt, N. C., Hooker, N.Y., Waful, N.Y., Bryant, Ill., Lowe, Ariz., and Blevins, Okla.

The day following, the latest batch of kriegies from the Italian front arrived. They were:

Lt. Col. Gaines Barron, Maj. Roy Irving, Capts. Robinson, Ferguson, Torrence and Bond, all Texans, Capts. Brown, Ill., and Cundiff, Okla., Lts. Williamson, Carlisle and Vaden, Texas, Lts. O'Brien, Haag, and Hannan, N. Y., Lts. Shirk, Okla., Young, Ohio, Hart, S. C., Livingston, Miss., Graham, Pa., Grimes and Brocker, N.J., Morrow, Wash., and Swanson, Calif.

The first page of the initial issue of *The Oflag Item* that appeared in November 1943 with four pages of news, humor and editorials. There were 15 monthly issues in all, the last in January 1945. The complete six pages of one typical issue, for October 1943, appears in Appendix C to this book.

"*Geprüft*" by the German translator assigned to keep an eye on such things. Not one word was ever changed, even in sly pieces that depicted the Germans as goons or harped on the persistent shortages of food, heat, and mail.

Every month I would be escorted by an armed guard to the print shop downtown, usually accompanied by Larry Phelan or Seymour Bolten, a New Yorker who spoke fluent German. There we would trim or expand the stories to fit each page since it was hard to judge their length without the use of a typewriter. Willi knew his business, however, and the only real problem we encountered was how to deal with his wife, a hopeless Nazi who always greeted us with a "Heil Hitler." We generally were able to ignore her.

Every kriegy got a copy of the finished product, so our circulation figures were a newspaperman's dream. They rose from about 225 copies for the first issue to 1,400 for the last, a 600-percent increase in 15 months.

New features were added regularly to our newspaper. A calendar of coming events was a standard item, as were humorous poems and news from home, lifted from our incoming mail and from interviews with new kriegies. Line drawings were possible, we found, so we used many of them from our two talented staff artists, Lts. Jim Bickers and Alexander Ross. Soon thereafter, photographs were added, leading to photo contests to choose the best-looking girl back home and later a best-looking baby. Bickers also did a sketch of the entire camp without the surrounding barbed-wire fence, which we used as part of the *Item* masthead.

Funny columns by Holder, Hancock, Rossback, and Phelan were especially popular. There were also editorials about camp doings and biographical sketches of some of the hard-working members of Col. Drake's staff. We even ran a "Literary Supplement" on two occasions, featuring short stories written by kriegies. The final issue in January 1945 included a special survey of all the camp activities and a report on who our "Oflagites" were, where they came from and their professional backgrounds.

Our biggest "scoop" by far came in the June 1944 issue, which came out on June 1. The lead story started off by stating that June 6 would be a "Red-Letter Day" at Oflag 64. And it was, of course. That turned out to be D-Day of the Normandy invasion. But the story referred to a planned celebration of the first anniversary of American POWs who had arrived just a year earlier. The celebration went off with much more enthusiasm than anticipated. The *Item's* story was considered the best reporting of coming events by everybody, including the Germans.

As we well knew, food and the lack of it were uppermost in our readers' minds, so there were frequent stories in that vein. One was about a kriegy who finally got a letter from home, six months delayed, which said his folks would be sending him a parcel of books and things he might need, ". . . but no food, because we understand you have plenty to eat from the Germans." Then there was the classic poem composed by Larry Phelan that went like this:

A KRIEGY SONNET

I dream as only captive man can dream,
Of life as lived in days that went before;
Of scrambled eggs and shortcake thick with cream,
And onion soup and lobster Thermidor;
Of roasted beef and chops and T-bone steaks,
And turkey breasts and golden leg or wing,
Of sausage, maple syrup, buckwheat cakes,
And chickens, boiled or fried or a la king.
I dwell on rolls or buns for days and days,
Hot cornbread, biscuits, Philadelphia scrapple,
Asparagus in cream or Hollandaise,
And deep-dish pies—mince, huckleberry, apple;
I long for buttered, creamy oyster stew,
And now and then, my pet, I long for you.

— Written to the lovliest girl in the world. LP

We couldn't, of course, write much about the escape attempts that were the subject of much kriegy speculation. But on one occasion, just after Lt. Col. Van Vliet and three other officers escaped and were recaptured and sentenced to 10 days of solitary confinement, we ran this squib on the sports page: "Good show, V.V. You and your team played heads-up ball against tough odds and bad breaks. You deserved to win. Better luck next time."

For a few months we had a famous war correspondent as a columnist for the *Item's* op-ed page. Larry Allen, a Pullitzer-prize-winning reporter for the Associated Press, had been captured when covering a British naval operation in the Mediterranean and sent as a civilian to Oflag 64. Larry amused all of us with tales of his journalistic high-jinks during the Wednesday night lecture series then being held in the Little Theater. He also gained quite a reputation for mooching cigarettes from his fellow prisoners, a fairly serious offense as cigarettes were in short supply and great demand. He was good at writing bio sketches for the camp paper, so I used him as often as possible.

Larry's big contribution during the six months he was with us was a news story that he would write every few days and post on the camp bulletin board. These stories were based on news that he gleaned from the German radio and newspapers, modified by what our secret radio reported from BBC in London. The result was always a fairly accurate report of war news, with the German slant deleted. This would carry his by-line and the underline, "Schubin Bureau of the AP." These news stories stopped only when Larry Allen was repatriated in May 1944 as a non-combatant civilian. Col. Drake was sent home at the same time with serious medical problems. Larry's departure left a hole in the camp's news coverage that was missed by all.

Keeping Current
With the War

7 After several months of publishing *The Item*, we felt we needed a daily news sheet with more than one story, more like the front page of an American daily newspaper with stories about the camp as well as the war. We thought that maybe we also needed maps and some news from home. Such a news sheet could be hand-lettered and pinned up every day on the White House bulletin board.

The first issue, aptly called *The Daily Bulletin*, appeared on May 8, 1944, just a month before the invasion of Normandy. It was an immediate success, about the same size and appearance as the front page of *The Washington Post*, my old employer. Its masthead was done in Old English printing just like the *Post's*. The big news, gleaned from the German radio and moderated by what we knew from BBC, was from the Russian front where the Soviets were about to break through at Sevastapol. Another piece covered some details of the German preparation for the expected allied invasion of France.

From then on, a lot of ingenuity went into the job of putting out a daily sheet. The YMCA somehow managed to produce sheets of paper large enough to resemble a newspaper. George Durgin manufactured most of the black ink used for headlines from soot scrapped from the inside of the ceramic heaters. I wrote the stories and hand-lettered them with my old fountain pen, which I miraculously still carried and which seemed to have an inexhaustible amount of ink. After I laid out the page, I would pencil in the headlines, which were then lettered in professionally by an engineering officer who knew how to print.

My friend, Seymour Bolten, who knew German well, was a key man on the staff. Every morning he would translate items from the German newspapers provided by the guards. Then he would give me a quick translation of the daily radio report put out by the German High Command. Seymour had an uncanny sense for appropriate news and a built-in sense of humor. He was therefore able to pick out endless faux pas put out by the serious-minded German propagandists. Larry Phelan covered local camp news and did theatrical reviews, always favorable of course. Ken Goddard did features.

New departments were added frequently. A column of news from America, mostly from interviews with newly arrived kriegies, soon became a regular weekly feature. Then we did a column called "International Roundup," with news from around the world not dealing with the war. A weekly box with planned camp activities became a standard item. War maps were run every few days, just to keep up with the German retreats. If, for example, German radio reported that the Russians were "repulsed with bloody losses at Minsk and Pinsk" and then the next week were repulsed with bloody losses at Mansk and Pansk 100 miles to the West, we simply wrote that the Reds had advanced 100 miles on the whole front. Our censor never questioned these truisms.

Once, however, we went a little too far. A German paper ran a photo that allegedly showed Nazi soldiers advancing through devastated farmland somewhere in Russia. In the foreground, several pigs were routing through the rubble. We clipped the picture and ran it with a caption saying "Swine on the Eastern Front." Our usually unimaginative censor, who had never blue-penciled anything we ran, could not let this go through unchallenged. With a scream of Teutonic anguish, he dashed through the gates and into the office of the German commandant. Minutes later, our Senior American Officer, then Col. Paul Goode, was visited by a delegation headed by *Oberst* Schneider. After a lengthy closed-door conference, they returned stiffly to their headquarters, leaving Col. Goode to handle the disciplinary action. He handled it well, and we promised to stick to more dispassionate reporting the next time.

We did keep one subtle takeoff from the German press in the slogan almost hidden under the masthead of *The Daily Bulletin*. It was patterned after that of

SOVIET DRIVE N. OF DANUBE RIVER NEARS KOMAROM, 50 Mi. FROM AUSTRIAN BORDER

U.S. Congressional Investigation of Blitz Is Expected

A U.S. Congressional investigation of the German surprise assault in the West is expected as soon as Congress reconvenes this month, according to an O.B. report today.

Discussions of "all phases and questions in connection with the German offensive" will lead the Congressional agenda.

Names of the U.S. officers responsible for the events have been demanded "without regard to rank."

The new Congress will sit on January 20, according to the German report.

HAPPY NEW YEAR TO ALL!

THE YEAR of hope and freedom and return to living opened today in Schubin while large-scale battles in the Ardennes Forest were raging to decide the fate of the crucial year of 1945

Russian Assaults in Hungary Combine Into Unified Attack

Russian assaults of the past few days have "flowed into a unified violent attack between Lake Platten and the south Slovakian border, ostdeutscher Beobachter reported today.

The main attack is driving along the railroads leading from Stuhlweissenburg and Budapest to Komarom, within 50 miles of the Austrian border.

North of the Danube bend, the Soviets are attempting to encircle from the southwest German forces still fighting East of the Gran River.

Cold Wave Hits U.S., Local Mercury Is 28°

A cold wave is now coming ⅔ of the U.S. with temperatures down as low as 24° below zero. In Schubin the temperature today is 28.4°.

Canada Sees Greatest Gold Rush of Its History, Stock Quotations Soar

Canada is now having the greatest gold rush in its history, according to a wall Street Journal report from Ottawa.

More than 300 new borings have been made. stock exchange quotations sometimes rise

as much as a dollar overnight because one boring has struck gold.

One gold firm rose from 20¢ to $10.75 on the Toronto exchange.

In Ontario province, 9000 prospector's rights were staked in 1944.

SIDELIGHTS

● BERNE reports that the Swiss federal laws against Communist activities will be lifted this month.

● IN 1944, the U.S. debt was raised 52 billion dollars to reach a total of 232 billions.

● ACCORDING to a Swedish report, the Russian government has decided to build a 500-mile gas pipeline from Saratow on the lower Volga south to Moscow.

JANUARY 1, 1945

U.S. Munition Plants Work Overtime

U.S. munitions workers have been asked to work today (New Year's Day) to meet the urgent need of munitions on the West Front.

"Room Service," Top-Notch N.Y. Comedy, Opens '45 Season on Oflag Stage

Fast-moving Broadway comedy greeted the new year here last night with the Oflag premier of John Shannan's production of "Room Service."

Well-acted, well-set and well-cast, the Doctor rang the bell as one

of the top three shows to hit the Schubin stage.

Starring in the comedy, which is to run throughout this week, are: Producer Hannan, Frank Maxwell, Bill Swanson, Gardner Summer, Siles Beilin, John Glendining, Wilbur Sharp, Danny Danide, John Cramer, Burrows.

A typical issue of *The Daily Bulletin*, this one dated January 1, 1945, and posted on the camp bulletin board that day, along with a special Radio Edition and a feature page.

the *Volkisher Beobachter*, the official Nazi party organ, which proclaimed: *"Freiheit und Brot"* or Freedom and Bread. Not to be outdone, our slogan read *"Freiheit und Weissbrot"* or "freedom and white bread"—both of which we wanted badly.

German guesswork always made for interesting reading in *The Bulletin.* Just before the D-Day invasion, German newspapers were predicting that Cherbourg was the likely allied target in France. One paper reported that Washington expected the war to end by July 1945, not far off from the actual date as it turned out.

Soon before the D-Day invasion, we started adding a second page to *The Bulletin* from time to time as a special radio edition. This page was to cover any late news heard over the daily afternoon radio broadcasts by the German High Command. It soon became a frequent practice, appearing on a slightly smaller page size and always with a war map to show where the action was. The actual invasion was especially hard for us to cover because we knew more about it than the German camp staff knew, thanks to The Bird, but we couldn't admit it. By midday there was a brief announcement on the German radio, and that was enough for us to come out with a two-page special edition, with a foot-high headline, "INVASION!" and maps and pictures of the broad invasion coast in France. Two days later the German radio finally came through with much detail on the allied landings, which we were then able to publish. The High Command was predicting more invasions yet to come on other fronts, so that much of the Nazi defensive force was being held back, just as Eisenhower had hoped. Deadpan, we also quoted the German radio's "Lord Haw-Haw" with his far-fetched explanation of just why the allied forces were not yet thrown back into the sea. It seemed that luring more troops ashore was part of a clever bit of Third Reich strategy.

While this crucial fighting was happening, we noted hints in the German press about what America's role would be in the postwar world. There apparently was great interest in Berlin in the U.S. plans for United Nations organization, and just what countries would be asked to belong to it. Maybe Germany would be left out in the cold.

The big Russian offensive that was building up at the same time during the summer of 1944 was of even greater interest to our readers, who figured correctly that the Soviet army was headed directly for Schubin and Oflag 64. Did they know we were here, or would they just shoot up everything in their path to

ROME FALLS

Americans Enter City; Germans Evacuate.

Rome has fallen.

German troops today evacuated the Italian capital "to save it from destruction."

American and British troops entered the city, goal of the Italian campaign, just nine months after the Allied landing in Italy.

The move climaxed a whirlwind offensive which began at Cassino on May 12 and drove 125 kilometers through strong German defenses in 25 days.

It marked the first time that Rome has been taken by an invading army since the middle ages.

The Reason

June 6:— German radio last night said that Pres. Roosevelt and Churchill had given their generals permission to destroy Rome if that were necessary for its capture. So "to save Rome" the Germans evacuated.

Radio Bleeds

Berlin propagandists last night claimed that the Americans conducted "an orgy of celebration and sham battle" in conquered Rome, "defacing" sections of the city.

Alibying the evacuation, they added, "they cannot point a finger in accusation at Germany for the ravages of Rome."

Americans Enter Rome

Our *Daily Bulletin's* Radio Edition scored a scoop when Rome was declared an open city and American forces marched in. The photo accompanying that story was originally a German newspaper picture of captured American troops, cleverly touched up by staff artist Bickers to make them look like armed GIs entering the city.

The death of German General Romel was big news to about 200 of the earliest Oflag 64 kriegies, who were captured by his famed *Afrika Korps*. An editorial in the next day's *Daily Bulletin* said that the general was greatly respected by the Americans and would be an irreplaceable loss to the Third Reich.

Berlin? So we covered every German report from the Russian front with maps showing how the German army was "falling back to new positions," closer and closer to us. The newspapers kept us well supplied, too, with grim photographs of German troops trudging through the mud and snow, back along the way they had driven so successfully four years before. On September 7, 1944, our "Special Radio Edition" reported the interesting news that the Russians had reached the last major town on our map before hitting Oflag 64. There, however, the big Russian push apparently stopped to regroup.

As winter came on, our news reports revealed more and more indications of the German forces in trouble on both east and west fronts. News photos focused many times on wounded German soldiers and wrecked German tanks and vehicles. Young German boys were being called up for military service in the "Hitler Youth" organizations. Civilian uprisings in occupied Europe were reported as "increased terrorist attacks." Nazi officials now referred to the German front as being "flexible."

Even with the war obviously approaching its military climax, the German press was featuring much nonmilitary news about America, and we, of course, reported it. The 1944 political campaign got big coverage with Roosevelt running for a fourth term. Eisenhower was quoted constantly. Much emphasis was placed on what the Germans said was Eisenhower's "five-point order of occupation" for running postwar Germany. The Dumbarton Oaks conference in Washington, called to set up a postwar United Nations, provoked great interest. German papers also played up the story of General George Patton's "slapping" a wounded American soldier. An unlikely story also described Americans taking over the Eiffel Tower in Paris.

The German magazine pieces about America were often good for a laugh. We devoted one feature to an article in *Die Wolke* that accused Texans of being "war profiteers" because so much of U.S. war industry was being located there instead of the industrial centers of New England and California. Another magazine showed a collection of German photos indicating that America was being run entirely by Jews—terrible people such as New York's Mayor La Guardia.

Sometimes the German press played it straight. We lifted a photo report from one Nazi magazine showing the emergency measures taken in order to feed people in bombed-out German cities. The photos gave a clear picture of how much damage was being done by allied bombing. How extensive the Russian

German Wounded Get Quick Aid

Speedy Evacuation Features Wehrmacht Medical Service

Like the Allies, the German Army has its unsung heroes in its first aid men shown awaiting

a call in the field. When they bring in a casualty to the aid station behind the front line, a medical officer is waiting to dress the injured's wound as rapidly as possible ...

... Evacuation follows by horse-drawn transport, by hospital plane or by motor ambulance (above)...

... to a field hospital where the wounded are bedded under canvas and receive a thorough examination to determine whether surgery or other medical treatment is needed.

SATURDAY, JANUARY 6, 1945

One of Ken Goddard's occasional feature pages, gleaned from one of the German magazines still being published during the war. It reflected the increasing number of German articles about their own casualties, as the number of killed and wounded rose rapidly after the Normandy invasion and the big Russian offensive.

push to the west had become was shown in a piece telling how some 350,000 "Black Sea Germans" were being evacuated back into Germany as Soviet territory was recaptured by the Russian army. While the German press rarely dealt with the war in the Pacific, we picked up one magazine piece on the Japanese war effort telling how they were starting to mobilize women and children, a sure sign of desperation on Tokyo's part.

From time to time, we would post special feature pages in place of the radio page. They covered all sorts of subjects, whatever we could dig up to give some background to the daily war news and maybe provide a laugh or two. Many of them were written around photo layouts and stories in the three German magazines which continued to publish on slick paper throughout the war. The talented American who turned out most of the special feature pages was Lt. Ken Goddard, aided by Lt. David Englander and occasionally by me. Ken had a special knack for layout and a curious mind about things European. Heavy-handed German propaganda was a favorite subject, which he would turn around to show how ridiculous it really was. Background stories on places where battles were currently going on were always well read. Photos of German starlets drew some attention as well.

One regular feature was the Sunday comic page. We made this up with cartoons from a German so-called "humor" magazine. Such humor was always heavy-handed, hard to understand, but usually funny in an obtuse way. We ran the cartoons with English translations of their captions to let our readers figure out what was so comic about them.

Most of the feature pages were in a serious vein, though. On the fifth anniversary of the war in 1944, for example, Ken did a detailed wrap-up of the vital role that American forces had played. From time to time, we did an overall look at how the war was going: disasters that Germans had admitted on the Russian front, the West front, the Italian front, the German home front, and the intensified air war.

Another of Ken's classics was headed, "Then and Now," with photos of victorious German forces sweeping over Europe in 1939, followed by others from German newspapers showing the retreating German troops going the other way. Ken also put together a large map for one feature page, showing where the Russian attacks were then underway along a 775-mile front. Other stories that we used indicated clearly how strong guerrilla activity was threatening the Nazis with disaster in the Balkans.

Surprisingly, the German media also provided the data that showed the price that Finland, Rumania, and Bulgaria had to pay to get out of the war. It sounded like a bargain to us, so we ran a page headed, "The Price of Peace." Another background piece went into some detail about what had happened in East Prussia, labeled by a German magazine as "a battleground for centuries." Our American officers were especially interested in a page of photos which we lifted from a German magazine showing a new Russian 120-mm mortar, described as "a favorite heavy weapon of the Soviet forces" with a range of some 6,000 meters.

For local news, one feature page was devoted to a coming sports field day with games of all kinds, featuring a number of kriegies who had been sports stars in their college days. Then we ran a feature of particular interest to old kriegies: a full rundown of U.S. Army demobilization plans as reported by a newcomer fresh from the States. The war with Germany was nearing its end, we figured, and if we survived Oflag 64, we wanted to know what would happen next. The report stated that four divisions not needed in the war against Japan were to be closed down and their troops returned to civilian life. A priority system would be established, based on the number of years served overseas, marital status, and so on. That was good news for kriegies who had been overseas a long, long time and were tired of being cold, hungry, and away too long.

The first thing that our avid readers looked for, however, was the daily weather report that winter. Temperatures were by now mostly well below freezing, both inside and outside our barracks. At one point on January 11, we reported a "heat wave" when the temperature rose nicely from 14 degrees to 32 degrees in the camp. The day before, there had been a record snowfall. Everybody was cold and we knew it. So then *The Bulletin* ran a regular feature displaying German starlets and entitled "It's a Cold, Cold Day in Schubin," along with posters telling of coming attractions at our own Little Theater. This, of course, was studied carefully by all our readership.

The Welcome Swede

8 A young Swedish civilian named Henry Soederberg turned out to be the best friend the American prisoners at Oflag 64 ever had. Henry was the representative of the International YMCA who visited the camp every two or three months and was responsible for bringing in tons of things that kept us relatively sane: thousands of books, baseballs, musical instruments, theatrical gear, Bibles, even paper and ink for the *Daily Bulletin*. He brought everything, in fact, except what we needed most—food.

Everybody called him Henry. He was one of only half a dozen foreigners permitted by the Germans to travel anywhere in occupied Europe and live off the local economy. Most kriegies thought he represented the Red Cross, but he didn't, he worked for the YMCA. Henry was well qualified to be a YMCA representative. He was a young man no older than most of our lieutenants and indeed a Christian, although he didn't make a big deal over it.

Henry hated the Nazis, but coped with them well enough to get our badly needed supplies to the camp by means of the overcrowded German rail lines from Sweden. He had several run-ins with suspicious German officials, traveled extensively on standing-room-only German trains, and survived a number of allied bombings while huddled in various German bomb shelters. For years, he made regular, periodic visits to all the American and British prison camps in Eastern Europe.

Henry Soederberg, the young YMCA representative from Sweden, who visited the camp often and brought in badly needed supplies, as he looked soon after the war.

Here is what he wrote in his wartime diary about his first visit to our camp on August 16, 1943:

"Today I have visited Oflag 64 for the first time, the camp for American officers. They are billeted in an old school where previously the Germans had kept British officers. There were several bold escape efforts made here in the past. For the time being, there are about 250 officers here. Most of them have been taken prisoner in North Africa at the end of the African campaign. They had been fighting against the German Field Marshal hero Erwin Rommel.

"I am getting an overwhelmingly fine reception. I am the very first visitor from the outside world, so they say. It seems that the joys of the officers are accentuated by the fact that already, some time before my visit, a big load of YMCA material had arrived from Geneva, which was a very quick delivery. This happened as a result of a request I had placed in Geneva for this camp after we had been informed by the German High Command that many American officers soon would arrive in Schubin. A very substantial need for equipment for cultural and leisure time activities was anticipated.

"The German commandant, *Oberst* Schneider, received me well. He says the Americans are *Schentlemen.* Their chief man of confidence, Colonel Drake, has gone away for the day for a medical checkup at a nearby hospital. But the commandant says that I shall find pleasure in meeting his stand-in, Lt. Col. John K. Waters. He points out that Waters is the son-in-law of General Patton, someone for whom the Germans seem to have the same kind of respect and admiration as they have in the reverse direction for their own Field Marshal Rommel.

"I find that John Waters and the officers I met today are very fine representatives of the United States. I am meeting a new kind of camp and different type of prisoners-of-war. Both the environment and the atmosphere are different are different from the many English camps I have visited, especially those with airmen. The Americans are not so arrogant toward the Germans as I am used to seeing in British camps. Perhaps the distance from here to home on the other side of the Atlantic Ocean is too long. The knowledge about European conditions and European geography seems to be very limited by many of those to whom I spoke. I do not think that these Americans are so much set to escape as are the British. However, I quickly find out that there is a very firm determination among the Americans to make the best of their captivity. The discipline in camp seems to be hard, thanks to Colonel Drake.

"I learned that John Waters is a man from West Point, a place with which I am not too familiar. I sat with Waters for two full hours. He is a very tall, athletic type of officer, perhaps 35 years old, with steel-gray eyes and an attitude that radiates both composure and determination, but also a deep amount of humanitarian feelings and friendliness. He tells me in well-controlled words what is going on in camp, about the situation at large, and I get the feeling that conditions are, on the whole, acceptable under the circumstances and that relations with the Germans are correct and harmonious. (A German security officer sits with us all the time and takes notes.)

"We then make a tour of the camp and met with various camp leaders. We walk up the stairs to the attic (of the White House) and I can see how they are arranging the space there for school and art classes. Many of the American prisoners are sitting there, sunk in their studies. The YMCA books already have arrived. They have a small library, which seems to be much appreciated. In one corner, a trio is playing first-class dance music. The trumpeter, so I am told, is a first-rate jazz musician. His name is Bob Rankin.

"In another part of the camp they are playing table tennis. They have made the table themselves, so they are not too fashionable. I promised them to place orders for the correct type of tables. In the room where the men sleep, I find many of them sitting, working with small models or hobby works of various kinds.

"Many of the men are coming up to see me. They are not shy at all; they tell me what kind of requests they have. I get the feeling of being a kind of Father

Christmas here. They have long lists, covering everything from pencils to type-writers and pianos, so I have to point out from time to time that there is a war going on. The transportation of goods is a real problem. Of course they understand this, laughingly.

"In a brick barrack out in the yard they are planning to build a theater. They need wood and planks and they need equipment of various kinds in order to get their theater going. I am speaking to the commandant about these things after the visit. He is promising, 'on my honor' he says, to do everything as quickly as possible in order to have a 'good camp.'

"One thing which really impresses me is that they already have a university of some kind going. But even with a staff of extremely good teachers, there is a great shortage of material for education."

Here are excerpts from Henry's later entries in his wartime diary:

"Sports life in Oflag 64 is flourishing but they need balls of various kinds. We are waiting with great tension for the tennis tables to arrive from Sweden, but at least they have been ordered."

"A Roman Catholic priest, Father Stanley Brack, a man with a neat beard and a velvet soft voice, now leads the well-attended religious services for both Catholics and Protestants. *Oberst* Schneider, the commandant, says that he is rather surprised about the activities by the Americans in the church field. He had never expected them to be that way, Goebbels is daily telling us something else.

"There is music en masse. Fine accordions have found their way into the camp. A piano teacher is conducting a class with several promising pupils. A choir was formed a couple of weeks ago and the group stood up in front of us and sang. It sounded fine, considering the short time they had been practicing."

"There is a professional radio man in the camp, Lt. Howard Holder. In civilian life he is a newscaster with an American radio station. He now has a regular radio program going over the camp loud speakers. You can hear this where are in the camp—music, lectures, information for the men and discussions. It seems to be a very much appreciated camp program. I understand that such activity must be typically American."

"I paid several more visits to Oflag 64 during this winter and spring, but even adventurous visits could become a kind of routine in the hectic life of a YMCA delegate, visiting two or three camps a week. I met many new and interesting American officers at every visit. Repeated contacts with them and messages to and from their homes in the USA created a kind of special friendship between us. I felt warmly toward them and they in turn seemed to like my visits. Here are a few extracts from my reports and letters to Sweden about Oflag 64 and its American prisoners:

"These American officers were throughout nice, stable young men with a fresh view on life. They were never stiff or stuffy; formalities were nothing for them. Their way of acting, therefore, especially to me since this was my first real contact with Americans, seemed to be somewhat nonchalant. They would be sitting at a table smoking cigarettes while we talked. What a difference from German soldiers standing at attention when I speak to them. There was something open in their characters which was very attractive."

"The camp has its own monthly newspaper. The editor is a professional in journalism, Lt. Frank Diggs. I think the *Oflag Item* is the very best camp magazine I have seen. Such a good variety of news and entertainment. It also mentions visits to the camp of the Red Cross and YMCA representatives."

At another visit to Oflag 64 that winter, Henry brought along two elderly YMCA officials and gave them an impromptu lesson in how to survive traveling in wartime Poland. The group arrived at Breslau where they were to get a train to Poznan, which was the mainline stop nearest to Schubin. At Breslau they found an enormous mass of people milling about the railroad station—soldiers, foreign workers, and prisoners being transported. A long wait ensued.

When the train finally arrived Henry told his elderly companions just what to do. One was to leap quickly through the first car door. The second was to jump over people to get through the second door. When the train approached, Henry crawled through a window of the car and held back the shoving, shouting, swearing mass of people until his two companions were able to get seats.

They gave him credit for good elbow work and spent the next 20 minutes watching the fighting going on along the station platform. The train finally departed and they devoted the rest of the night to taking turns holding the compartment's window closed that persisted in falling open at irregular intervals.

Around 5 a.m. they arrived at Poznan. There were no taxis or buses, so they walked through the town carrying their heavy luggage to the hotel where reservations had been made for them a week earlier. All the rooms were occupied, however. Henry took the manager aside, threatened him, bribed him, and lectured him—nothing worked. There were no rooms. So they sat and dozed in the lobby for several hours until two rooms were evacuated by several Nazi officials. After getting two hours' sleep, they returned to the Poznan train station for another train trip, this one on a rundown local Polish train.

Upon arrival in the little Polish town of Schubin they were met by a fat German officer driving a horse-drawn cart. He took them to a small hotel, where they recuperated for a couple of hours before walking to the high steel gates of Oflag 64.

In addition to Oflag 64, Henry serviced another major camp for American officers, Stalag Luft 3 in northern Poland. This camp was for shot-down U.S. and British airmen. It was a much larger prison camp than Oflag 64 and contained about ten times as many prisoners. It was located not far away at the town of Sagan.

The American pilots and crew who were shot down over Germany and confined at Luft 3 were, in general, described sometimes as a "cantankerous, rebellious, and unhappy lot." The camp was divided into six separate compounds, each with its own hierarchy of senior officers, its own doctors, chaplains, barracks, and sports area of sorts. Contact between them was forbidden, except for the senior American officer, Brig. Gen. Arthus Vanaman. The only American general to become a prisoner of the Germans, Vanaman had been aboard a bomber as an observer when it was hit by anti-aircraft fire. He and a British colonel, plus an Australian officer named Wilson, were allowed to visit all six compounds. So, of course, was Henry.

Like Oflag 64, this neighboring camp was tightly organized and full of intense activity. It was largely for flying officers, but had high-ranking noncoms as well. Even though they had to put up with roughly the same shortages of food, shoes, and warm clothing, there was a great effort made to keep everybody as busy as possible. The Y had already sent in some shipments of books and athletic gear, so each compound had a small library and ball field. In some compounds, the prisoners had built rudimentary theaters as well and had put on one or two amateurish but enthusiastic theatrical performances.

The Brits had been there longer, and had preempted the ball fields much of the time for frantic games of soccer and occasional cricket. The Americans stuck mostly to baseball and touch football as the YMCA equipment arrived.

Henry was most impressed by the elaborate classroom activity at Stalag Luft 3. There were daily classes in languages, with most kriegies trying to learn at least some German in case their escape plans worked out. All sorts of university-level subjects were being taught as textbooks became available, drawing on camp talent to provide often highly qualified teachers. Many airmen, particularly the British prisoners who had been penned up for three or four years, could take all of the courses required for a college degree here. Then there were art classes and musical groups that ranged from symphony to jazz. Classical music concerts were broadcast with records and loudspeakers supplied by the Y. It could have been a good life if it were not for certain drawbacks.

The fact is that prison life there, as at Oflag 64, was grim despite all efforts to make it passable. The young flyers were hungry from morning to night. They devoted much of their time to trying to extend their meager rations. When Red Cross parcels were several weeks late, as was often the case, they subsisted on the German ration of half-rotten potatoes, black bread, barley and occasional turnip jam. The regular meals the Germans provided consisted of only hot water for breakfast, a weak cabbage soup for lunch and whatever was available with a potato for supper.

Unlike the Oflag 64 kriegies, the airmen at Luft 3 were attired in all sorts of clothing—made-over pieces of uniforms, some old sweaters, and "long johns" when they could get them, with as many layers of clothes as each man could scrounge or swap for. Sometimes khaki scarves appeared in a Red Cross shipment, and these were quickly made into odd-looking hats to keep the ears warm. This was a luxury greatly prized in the unheated camps of northern Poland. Wooden clogs were worn by many at this camp, who claimed that they were surprisingly warm and dry, even though not very practical for playing baseball. Washing clothes was a special problem, as the available cold water removed little of the accumulated dirt and grease. So home-made washing machines were invented and widely used, consisting of a small tin can inserted into a larger one and both nailed to any available stick. Hot water was occasionally rationed out by the cookhouse, which helped immeasurably.

There was no privacy at Stalag Luft 3, which bothered many of the prisoners. The only place in the entire camp that a kriegy could call his own was his bunk. This consisted of a paper mattress filled with wood shavings, supported by four to six bed boards, and covered by two thin blankets. In the dead of winter, the lack of indoor heat caused many of the hungry men to stay in bed most of the time just in order to stay warm.

Many of the shot-down flyers had been badly burned or wounded and thus were being treated in the camp hospitals, usually by captured American doctors. More than a few of the young prisoners succumbed to nervous breakdowns as a result of being shot down and captured. And for many, the uncertainty, boredom and discomforts of prison life created moods of depression that would come and go. This was an occupational hazard that Henry's aid group was trying to prevent.

Henry thought the longing for freedom seemed to be especially strong among these airmen. There were constant efforts to escape. As he noted after the war, "there were no more clever diggers of tunnels in the whole of Germany during the war then the Air Force officers in Stalag Luft 3. I can readily subscribe to that." It was from this camp that the famous "Great Escape" took place about a year later.

From Luft 3, Henry traveled to two more of the seven camps that housed American airmen—Stalag Luft 6 near Memel in East Prussia and Stalag Luft 7 outside Kreutzburg in Upper Silesia. He found these two even more crowded but otherwise in about the same condition as Luft 3. In all, there were forty thousand American and British prisoners in these seven airmen's camps by the end of the war, all of them officers or ranking noncoms, thus not permitted to work and badly in need of something to occupy their minds.

During the bitter cold winter of 1943–44, Henry made the rounds of the working camps for enlisted men, known as *commandos* nearby, where British and American GI prisoners were held in small groups to labor at various farms, offices, and factories in that part of Poland. He traveled with an English-speaking German security officer on local trains that often had no passenger cars attached. They frequently rode in boxcars, or cargo compartments or on open flat cars to some small town near their destination. Then they would walk long stretches to the small *commandos*, carrying their luggage with them. There Henry would be especially welcome, as many of the prisoners had been working for years in such out-of-the-way spots with no real contact with the outside world.

At one typical working *commando* they visited, there were only thirty-six English prisoners. During the day, they would be off working on a German-run farm; then they would gather at their little camp at night. Henry joined them one evening and listened to their individual problems, one by one. After a simple meal of toast and tea, someone brought out an accordion and soon all of them including Henry and the German guard were singing away. Before leaving the next morning, Henry promised to send them some books and a Swedish record-player with some records to go with it.

The largest working *commando* contained some eight hundred men, whom he visited later. At that time, they had nothing to entertain themselves with during the evening hours. But then their shipment of aid materials arrived and Henry was treated like Santa Claus. It included some five hundred books, instruments to start their own orchestra, a supply of records and record-players, plus cards and other indoor games.

On his rounds to the other major prison camps in this part of the world, Henry discovered that most were far different than the Anglo-American camps. The treatment, the attitudes, and the needs were often worlds apart. The most pitiful prisoner of war camp in Europe, he concluded, was the one he visited next. This was Stalag VIII-BZ at Teschen in Upper Silesia, where thousands of Slavs, Belgians, and Poles were cooped up, and with a special compound for sick Russian prisoners. The barracks were very old and overcrowded, and the stench was almost overpowering. He was escorted through the miserable unheated quarters where laundry was hanging everywhere and prisoners were sitting or lying dejectedly on their bunks.

Most of the prisoners had been there for a long time and had more or less lost their will to live. Only the Poles seemed to keep busy doing anything when they were not out on working commandos. There were hardly any requests for the things that the Y might provide. Henry tried to interest the Slav camp leader in starting a camp newspaper, in an attempt to revive some spirit, but to no avail.

Worst of all was the big Russian hospital compounds. The German commandant gave Henry permission on one visit to go into the Russian sector, accompanied by a Soviet doctor. He describes his visit in his diary like this: "It's a frightening sight. It is very dark, very dirty, and has a sour, stinking atmosphere and smell that is nearly putting me to sleep. Everywhere I look there are only shades of people, pale and worn out. Most of them are lying around or sitting on beds in their dirty coats. In every corner, people are coughing.

Very sick, tired glances are following me. They are asking themselves who I could be.

"The doctor explains, 'Most of them have tuberculosis. We have nothing to treat that with. If we only had some help from the Red Cross or the YMCA perhaps . . .' The German security officer who accompanies me then speaks up. Well, we would like to do something for them but the German High Command does not permit it.

"The Russians are dying en masse daily. I can see several dead bodies lying in a corner. These are today's victims. 'Tomorrow we will carry them away,' they tell me. Obviously their families will never know what happened to them or where they died."

Ironically, the prisoners of war who, next to the Russians, lived in the most miserable conditions, Henry reports, were those of Germany's old ally, Italy. After the capitulation of Badoglio in the late summer of 1943, camps all over Germany were suddenly filled up with Italian soldiers. Hitler considered them traitors to the Third Reich and ordered that they be given a hard time.

With very limited rations of food and horribly overcrowded conditions, the Italian prisoners were then given the option of returning to active duty and fighting for Hitler against the Russians or staying in their filthy prison camps. That German stratagem failed, however, and about 98 percent of the Italian prisoners elected to stay where they were despite the inhuman conditions and starvation diet. Henry's aid group was not permitted to bring in any material help for the Italians, as a means of exerting more pressure on those sad prisoners.

While Henry Soederberg was doing so much to preserve our sanity at Oflag 64, he was checking regularly with most of the prisoner of war camps in Eastern occupied Europe and thus saw close-up how Germany's prisoners were faring. As the war grew in intensity, the Nazi element appeared to be taking over running the camps. Soon every proposal from the War Prisoners Aid, every application, every practical action for the good of any prisoners of war in Europe had to be approved by the inner circles of the Gestapo. So it was that Henry, who had to deal with them for the good of all of us, begin to hate the Nazis with a purple passion.

Bad Treatment Gets Worse

9 After D-Day, with paratroopers dropping in the wrong places, infantry units pushing ahead too fast, and the Germans giving their all at the Battle of the Bulge, the number of captured Americans rose rapidly. This increased the head-count at Oflag 64 about four-fold, at a time when the Nazi treatment of all prisoners worsened considerably.

The first evidence of the German crack-down came when we were all held in an *Appell* formation for several hours one day while the German guards went through our lockers and confiscated uniforms and personal equipment from them all. This provided the Germans with a large array of American uniforms which were later used to camouflage German troops. On specific orders from Hitler, all benefits for prisoners of war were then to stop and POWs were to be treated like any other prisoners. These orders complicated life in many ways. Food rations were to be cut further, so that Americans would eat "no better than German civilians," and Red Cross parcels were deliberately withheld and stored within the camp.

Four of my closest kriegy friends fell victim to this new attitude in a big way. Lts. George Durgin, Seymour Bolten, Jack Rathbone, and Pat Teel were being escorted under guard to the railway station in order to get medical treatment in the nearby town. Outside the gate, they were ordered by the guard to walk in the gutter instead of the sidewalk. Seymour said that they were American officers, not criminals, and they refused to walk in the gutter. "OK," the guard replied, "then walk on the sidewalk." They did so, but when they returned to camp later, the guard told the German commandant what had happened and the *Oberst* queried Berlin to ask for directions.

Hitler replied that the Americans had disobeyed a direct order from a German soldier and, thus, should be shot. First, however, there must be a trial. The four kriegies were taken to a German army court in another town and were assigned a German lawyer as their defender. He made a good case of it, citing the Geneva Convention and German officer traditions. Then, much to everybody's surprise, the Americans were acquitted and sent back to camp.

This acquittal infuriated Hitler, who immediately ordered another trial. A retrial was held on January 25, 1945, without the Americans being present, as the retrial happened five days after the camp had been evacuated. This time, all four officers received the death sentence, but fortunately, they were by then all off on the long march to liberation and so lived to survive the war.

In another case, Lt. James R. Schmitz, our assistant adjutant, was in the camp office alone when he was approached by two German guards who were about to post some anti-escape posters on the office wall. Schmitz considered the posters insulting to American officers as they accused our government of "resorting to gangster warfare up to and within the frontier of the Fatherland." So he requested them to wait until he could contact our SAO. He was unable to reach the colonel and brought back Lt. Col. Schaefer instead, who discussed the posters with the guards. As they were leaving, Lt. Schmitz stood in the doorway in token protest. When one of the *Unteroffiziers* approached and touched Schmitz, he immediately got out of the way. Nevertheless, the American was accused of blocking the doorway, and Lt. Col. Schaefer was accused of "interfering with the functions of the German Reich." They were both tried in December 1944, found guilty, and sentenced to death. The camp was evacuated the next month before the sentence could be carried out, however, so they too survived.

Strangely, despite all the harassment and the near-starvation diet, there was not much sickness in the camp other than colds, flu and frostbite. The hospital was full of new prisoners recovering from wounds received in combat, but the old prisoners were seldom sick. The medics speculated that perhaps the few vegetables that we were able to grow in our two-acre garden may have warded off the scurvy-like diseases that might have been expected. Nonetheless, our physical condition deteriorated as time went by. For the first time, men sometimes fainted from weakness after standing for a long time at *Appell*. One kriegy, Capt. Richard H. Torrance, Jr., from Waco, Texas, died of a heart attack while standing at *Appell* and was given a fine military funeral at the camp chapel.

Personally, I had only one health-related visit to the hospital. That visit resulted from a bad toothache that kept getting worse every day. I spent a lot of time nursing it with my chin up against a ceramic stove, but with no success. Then somebody said that two dentists had just arrived in camp, so I rushed over to try to have a wisdom tooth pulled. No problem, they said, except they had no dental equipment at the time. Somewhere in camp, they found a suitable pair of pliers. Without novocaine, it took about 20 minutes to extract it, but the ailing tooth did get pulled and this solved my problem.

The change in our treatment began almost immediately after D-Day in 1944 when Hitler gave more influence in POW matters to the SS and the Gestapo and less to the German regular army generals. Of the German staff at the camp, *Hauptman* Zimmerman, who was apparently the only devoted Nazi party member, suddenly had great influence as the German security officer. His word became law. He made it clear that there would be no more "coddling" of the American prisoners. The occasional walks outside the camp were stopped at once. Saluting by the German officers was ended and supposedly was to be replaced by a Hitler straight-arm *Heil.*" Some of the staff officers fudged this a bit with a half-salute, which seemed to pass muster.

Parcels from home, which had been allowed with an 11-pound limit every two months to each prisoner, stopped coming almost completely. Mail from home, which had been coming only a month or two late, suddenly arrived three or four months late, if at all. Red Cross parcels, the most important of all, simply stopped coming, even though stockpiles of them were found later outside the camp. Zimmerman explained that this situation was caused by the constant bombing of German rail lines by those cursed Americans.

After the murder of the 50 escaped prisoners from Stalag Luft 3, our tunnel project was ordered by the SAO to be closed down, so most of the escape attempts were ended until the camp evacuation in January 1945. The Germans posted a warning on our bulletin board that escaped prisoners would no longer

7 January 45

My darling Evy:- Another assortment of
repatriates left here this week for God's
country. One of them, Lt. Frank Maxwell,
will drop you a line shortly on the state
of affairs over here. Tell Rae that
he will call the old man too-the hired
help should be interested in his tales.
I've just finished reading a screwball
little book you might enjoy-at least
it appealed to my depraved sense
of humor: "Jitter Hum" by Robert
Germann. Also several heavy tomes
that you wouldn't enjoy at all so I
won't bother to list. Mail being very
erratic here, nearly half of your letters haven't shown up yet so tell me
again: 1.)Did my bedroll and locker ever
get home, 2.)Did you get up to see
Ginnie last May, 3.) Did you ever collect that Silver Star last winter, 4.)
What happened to Bob Case, and
5.)Do you still love me ?? My congratu-
lations to Bill Wright for joining an up-
and-coming outfit. We've been reading
a lot about its recent reshuffle and
doin's here lately. I've been seriously
thinking about getting attached to
Nelson's or Archy's departments in
a traveling & writing capacity someday.

If this appeals to you too, you might start
investigating their post-war plans. Give
my love to Mother and Dad and take care
of yourself for me. Hold tight. All my love, Frank

Kriegsgefangenenpost

Mit Luftpost
Nach Nord Amerika
Chg: 40 R.G.

Taxe perçue _____ RM 44 RPF

„Mit Luftpost
Par avion"

Mrs. J. Frank Diggs

Empfangsort: *Linthicum Hts.*
Straße: _____
Kreis: *Md.*
Land: *U.S.A.*
Landesteil (Provinz usw.)

3
Geprüft
Oflag

11972
U.S. CENSOR

Gebührenfrei!

Deutschland (Allemagne)

Lager-Bezeichnung: M.-Stammlager XXI b Oflag 64
Gefangenennummer:
Vor- und Zuname: *2023*
Absender: *Lt. J.F. Diggs*

Prisoners were allowed to write three form letters and four postcards home each month, each of them closely censored at both ends. Here is a typical letter as received by my wife, with the required notation, "Airmail to North America, 40 cents" in German and the censor's stamp, "Gepruft, Oflag 64." It was delivered a few weeks later. Mail from home, considered much more important, usually took months to arrive.

To all Prisoners of War!

The escape from prison camps is no longer a sport!

Germany has always kept to the Hague Convention and only punished recaptured prisoners of war with minor disciplinary punishment.

Germany will still maintain these principles of international law.

But England has besides fighting at the front in an honest manner instituted an illegal warfare in non combat zones in the form of gangster commandos, terror bandits and sabotage troops even up to the frontiers of Germany.

They say in a captured secret and confidential English military pamphlet,

THE HANDBOOK OF MODERN IRREGULAR WARFARE:

". . . the days when we could practise the rules of sportsmanship are over. For the time being, every soldier must be a potential gangster and must be prepared to adopt their methods whenever necessary."

"The sphere of operations should always include the enemy's own country, any occupied territory, and in certain circumstances, such neutral countries as he is using as a source of supply."

England has with these instructions opened up a non military form of gangster war!

Germany is determined to safeguard her homeland, and especially her war industry and provisional centres for the fighting fronts. Therefore it has become necessary to create strictly forbidden zones, called death zones, in which all unauthorised trespassers will be immediately shot on sight.

Escaping prisoners of war, entering such death zones, will certainly lose their lives. They are therefore in constant danger of being mistaken for enemy agents or sabotage groups.

Urgent warning is given against making future escapes!

In plain English: Stay in the camp where you will be safe! Breaking out of it is now a damned dangerous act.

The chances of preserving your life are almost nil!

All police and military guards have been given the most strict orders to shoot on sight all suspected persons.

Escaping from prison camps has ceased to be a sport!

This warning that any escaping prisoners were liable to be shot was posted on the camp bulletin board after the 50 escaping airmen from Stalag Luft 3 were murdered by Hitler, as portrayed in *The Great Escape*. This was a clear violation of the Geneva Convention, which provided for not more than a one-month imprisonment for any recaptured prisoner of war.

get the permitted maximum of 30 days punishment in solitary, but they would be considered potential gangsters and thus subject to being shot if recaptured. What was left of the observance of the Geneva Convention at Oflag 64 was dead.

The German warning, posted on our bulletin board, put it this way: "Escaping is no longer a game . . . Germany is determined to safeguard her homeland, and especially her war industry and provisional centers for the fighting fronts. Therefore it has become necessary to create strictly forbidden zones, called death zones, in which all unauthorized trespassers will be immediately shot on sight. Escaping prisoners of war, entering such death zones, will certainly lose their lives. They are therefore in constant danger of being mistaken for enemy agents or sabotage groups."

The Germans also began a series of constant searches of our quarters to confiscate anything that was not permitted under the new camp regulations. These searches were carried out quite efficiently by two of the guards, whom the kriegies called the Ferret and the Weasel. They would go through all of the lockers in a barracks and remove any empty Red Cross tin cans, which might be used for tunnels, or more than a specified amount of tobacco and food that might be used for bribery, in addition to any spare clothing that they found. On a few occasions, a Gestapo search party would come into the camp and check to see that the Ferret and the Weasel had not missed anything.

As winter came on, we began to see groups of refugees moving west on the *Adolph Hitler Strasse* beside the camp. The big Russian offensive was on. The Germans who had been living so well in occupied Poland were now leaving in droves. The refugee traffic grew steadily, with lines of horse-drawn wagons interspersed with trucks and families walking often four-abreast. Sometimes large droves of horses would go by, apparently taken from the large farms now being evacuated. The German press inadvertently helped step up this flow of refugees by reporting case after case of Russian "atrocities" against German families in Poland. We were, of course, directly in the path of the oncoming Russian drive. We speculated at length about whether the Soviets would recognize us as Americans and their wartime allies, or whether the might just blast away at Oflag 64, believing it was another German military post, when they got here. No one was quite sure just how the Russian front-line troops operated.

Mail from home, probably the most important factor in a prisoner's morale, now was being sharply cut back. Most letters were taking about 100 days to arrive, rather than four or five weeks. Several letters we received were more than a year late. The record was held by one kriegy who received six letters in one day, all over a year old. All letters were now heavily censored with words, sentences, and paragraphs blacked out with ink. There was strong evidence that mail which had arrived was being stored in camp without being distributed, for weeks and months at a time. In my case, after the camp was evacuated in January 1945, Seymour Bolten, left behind as an interpreter, uncovered a large stack of undelivered mail that included 26 letters to me from my wife.

Hunger, always uppermost in the prisoners' minds, grew more constant and emphatic as the rations were cut back. From October 10, 1944, to December 3, 1944, no Red Cross parcels were delivered to the camp, and the men suffered accordingly. The doctors were concerned and checked

Birds of a Feather

Don't be hasty, Murgatroyd — mebbe a horse'll come by!

German wartime black bread, which appeared to be mostly sawdust, was widely acclaimed to be about as edible as horse droppings. Though tasteless, it did contain some nourishment. This subtle cartoon is from The *Item*.

the weight of everyone weekly from October 20 to November 15. Dr. Peter Graffagnino, an expert on nutrition who taught that subject at the camp, figured that during that period the average loss was nine pounds per man. Among the old kriegies, the total weight loss at the camp was often 30 to 50 pounds.

The doctors reported that the German ration by this time had dropped to this average daily amount:

- Meat   35.7 grams
- Cooking oil   9.7 grams
- Barley   25 grams

- Cabbage   200 grams
- Dried vegs   6.2 grams
- Margarine   21.4 grams
- Cheese   4.5 grams
- Potatoes   353 grams
- Carrots   100 grams
- Bread   318 grams

Clothing became scarce, too. Before D-Day, the Red Cross had brought in enough American Army clothes to provide each man with two winter uniforms, one American overcoat, some underwear, socks and shoes, and sometimes jackets. By November 1944, the Germans demanded that all POWs turn in all but one uniform. They also demanded our field jackets, which were at first refused. As a result, the guards came through the barracks with fixed bayonets and fired their rifles into the air, forcing the men to give up their jackets. The original excuse for all this confiscation was that clothing was needed for new POWs, but officers arrived wearing British, French and even Russian uniforms, which were never replaced by American equivalents.

By now the camp was getting crowded. The number of kriegies had about doubled in a few months. All the barracks were filled. The mess hall had to provide second sittings. The Little Theater was too small for all to attend, so that four performances were required for each play. The *appells* which had been held behind the White House until September, were moved up to the athletic field. There was little elbow room for the prisoners. Every place was crowded—the library, the mess hall, the White House, all barracks and athletic areas. There was no more privacy to be had.

Despite these growing handicaps, most of the Americans were coping well. An assessment by the Army's Military Intelligence Service after the war reported it this way:

"The morale of the men, especially after 'D-Day,' was exceedingly high. This spirit was reflected in the monthly publication known as *The Oflag Item*, which was issued from November 1943 to January 1945. By making light of the 'kriegy woes' and reviewing the month's activities in the vein of a collegiate newspaper, as easy air of comradeship was developed. The 'Little Theater of

Schubin College' was a huge success. POWs produced a total of eight three-act plays, all of which were former Broadway hits. They also produced seven one-act plays, eight musical reviews and one original three-act play. In addition to these activities, the men took part in many types of sports. A league was formed for baseball and softball enthusiasts as well as basketball players. Thus, men kept their morale high by keeping occupied."

Escape Across Russia

10 Every prisoner dreams of escaping. My chance came when the Russian army, in its massive drive across Poland, drew within earshot of Oflag 64. As the sound of artillery fire became constant and grew louder, the Germans decided to march all 1,400 of their American officers back into Germany before the camp was overrun. This was decided in January 1945, the dead of winter in northern Poland.

It was bitter cold and had been snowing hard when the whole camp, except for about 80 of the wounded who were then in the hospital, bundled up and shuffled out through the finally opened gates. Based on notes that I started when the march began, here is what happened next:

January 21, 1945—SCHUBIN, Poland

The long column headed south under heavy German guard, each man carrying all of his possessions, including an entire Red Cross food parcel. I was somewhere in the middle, sharing an old sled with Lt. Nelson Tacy. The snow was nearly two feet deep and the stuff had been blowing horizontally. Artillery fire sounded fairly close. The Russians were headed our way.

The POW column itself is headed back into Germany, we're told. Guards are looking grim and a bit nervous. Forced marches are promised ahead. Tacy and I are hauling our collective gear on an ancient six-foot Polish sled, which we found hidden in the White

House basement long ago. At least we're now outside the barbed wire after being behind it and trying to get out for 18 months.

With slow but steady marching, we covered around 24 kilometers by night-fall. It was tiring and very cold, but no casualties are reported as yet. We found no chance to get away either. We're bivouacked now in a large Polish barn.

January 22—POLANOVA, Poland

Starting up just after dawn, the column trudged along all day, covering some 23 kilometers. The snow has stopped falling, thank God, but it's still cold, about 12 degrees, we figure. We've been testing out the guards, hoping to get away. A couple of kriegies nearly made it by slipping into a culvert, but the Germans found them and proved to be very trigger-happy, so that tactic didn't work.

At nightfall, our weary group was split up and assigned to several farm buildings to bed down. Tacy and I wound up in a loft above an enclosed pig sty. The hogs were noisy all night; yet, it turned out to be the warmest place around.

January 23—CHARLOTTENBERG, Poland

The column got a late start this morning because of a heavy snowfall overnight and the mysterious, temporary disappearance of most of the guards. They all returned before we realized they had gone, and they made up for lost time by pushing us at a steady, tiring pace all day. The Russians seem to be getting closer now, with heavy artillery sounding almost constantly.

We halted for the night at a large compound, which, includes a massive dairy barn, surrounded by a high barbed-wire fence. The whole group was ordered to bed down in the haylofts overhead after receiving rations that consisted of some hard German black bread. Guards were posted at the entrance and corners of the compound, but not inside.

This situation was what we'd been hoping for, so Tacy and I decided to try the escape plan that we had rehearsed so often. We each put on our escape costume, which made Nelson look like a disreputable Polish worker and me resemble a German guard, with a homemade cloth "helmet" and a stick of wood carved to slightly resemble a rifle. Thus attired, in the dim light of dusk, Tacy slowly pulled our loaded sled across the compound to an unlighted far end, while I followed and swore at him from time to time in low German. It was supposed to look like a typical work detail—and it worked.

A German guard called out something to us once, but then paid no further attention. We made it to the far rear fence undetected. Tacy climbed carefully to the top of the 10-foot barbed-wire fence. I hoisted the sled up to him, and we manhandled it over the top. It dropped with a thud in the deep snow on the other side. Then I climbed up and we both jumped down after it.

There were no shouts or shots, just a nice, quiet snowfall. So we resumed our masquerade. Tacy pulled the sled down the road and I followed behind—just in case. The first person we saw, fortunately, was a lone Pole hurrying to get home. He knew no English, but I soon convinced him with my fractured German that we were Americans who needed a place to hide. Our new friend knew of just such a place: a farmhouse only a few kilometers away where a member of the local Polish underground lived.

We thanked this gentleman profusely and mushed on, with both of us pulling the sled for an hour or two through the deep snow. There, just as he described it, was the indicated farmhouse, or at least we hoped it was. We went up and knocked. The door opened just a crack. We explained in poor German that we were American officers and would like to come in. With that, the door was flung open and we were pulled inside, along with the sled.

It was a large Polish family who welcomed up vigorously. Momma produced something for us to eat, which was more than welcome. Then everybody wanted to talk, which went on by kerosene lamplight until a late hour, with the help of many gestures and my pocket German dictionary. Finally Tacy and I, as guests of honor, retired to a small but genuine featherbed—the first real bed either of us had slept on in more than two years. It felt great.

January 24–28—WIRSITZ, Poland

We stayed with the Dudziak family for five days and got to know them well. They were a fine, fearless, generous, and wonderful farm family, living in a two-and-a half room fairly primitive farmhouse located near Wirsitz. The farm consisted of probably 20 or 30 acres. Father Dudziak, in his 50s, is a quiet, weather-beaten farmer, a member of the local anti-German underground group. He took in everything but said little. Momma is a tiny, energetic woman who stations herself by a working spinning wheel in the living room and rules the family with an unquestioned iron hand. There are two boys in their early 20s, another about 15 and a quiet little girl of perhaps 12.

They flatly refused to let us stay in the barn, as we asked. Despite the obvious danger to the family, they said we must stay in the house. This arrangement was almost their undoing, as German patrols were seen in the area the next day, possibly looking for us. Later that day, in fact, two German soldiers came to the door and asked if they had seen any Americans. At the time, Tacy and I were standing back on either side of the door with improvised clubs in hand, hoping to be able to clobber them if they came in. But our Polish friends assured them, however, that they had seen no *Amerikanishers*, so the Germans left without entering.

On the second evening, many of the Polish neighbors came visiting, and we were properly introduced. They reported that other Americans had hidden out in the hayloft when the column pulled out, but the Germans returned and began shooting into the hay. With that, the kriegies tumbled out and were marched away. Tough. We haven't heard of any other escapees yet.

Each day, more neighbors dropped in, often bringing us small amounts of hoarded food. None could speak English, although several had relatives around Detroit. We found that the Poles were more apprehensive of the approaching Russians than of the retreating Germans. The Dudziak family had survived six years of rather barbaric treatment under the Germans and were determined to stay here and keep operating their small farm. We discovered that they were deeply religious, practicing Catholics, but vehemently anti-Semitic. Surprisingly, they blamed many of their country's problems not on Hitler but on the Polish Jews, who couldn't have had anything to do with Poland's troubles.

Time after time, we heard the wistful notion expressed that somehow the U.S. Army would come to the aid of Poland after Germany was defeated and before Russia could take over the country. We asked our hosts to please not to count on it. But this appeared to be the only hope they had for Poland's future.

January 27—WIRSITZ, Poland

Today we went out and met the Russians. Our Polish friends reported that there was fighting in the nearby town this morning, which we could plainly hear, and that the Russians were pouring in. So we said farewell to the Dudziaks, distributed part of our small hoard of Red Cross cigarettes to the family, and trudged through the deep snow for several kilometers to town.

From a distance, the advancing Russians army looked like nothing but small groups of unrelated units of men and vehicles dotting the landscape and all moving slowly in the same general direction. There are horse-drawn sleighs moving cross-country, mounted cavalry scouts investigating off-road buildings, a few tanks roaring down the main highway, some familiar-looking army trucks and squads of infantry carefully reconnoitering the town. Interspersed with all this are individual artillery pieces pulled by horses or trucks, moving down the highway and occasionally swinging into position to fire a few rounds.

We weren't at all sure what our reception would be. Tacy and I were wearing old U.S. Army uniforms, G.I. overcoats, and homemade hats that we had sewed together for warmth out of old Red Cross scarves. We hoped that we didn't look too German, but we couldn't be sure.

As it turned out, the first Russian soldier we met face-to-face was a ragged artilleryman who had just pulled his stuck, horse-drawn gun out of a ditch. I approached him and said, *Amerikanski*. He considered this for a few moments, then removed his glove, stuck out a grimy, calloused paw, and said, *Ruski*. We shook hands solemnly all around and he departed.

Then, a horse-drawn sleigh cut across the fields toward us. We found ourselves facing a grim, suspicious Russian colonel, who obviously wanted to know just who the hell we were. His batman, a lad of not more than 15 years who sat next to the driver, held a Russian burp-gun pointed straight at our heads. We quickly tried *Amerikanski* and showed the colonel our U.S. Army identify cards. No reaction. So we tried a few words in English, then French, Spanish and even German—our entire repertoire. He looked at the ID again carefully and said something that sounded like French. Then he waved us on. After that, we just yelled *Amerikanski* any Russians nearby and they always took our word for it.

The next bunch to move up were Mongolian horsemen, straight out of a *Genghis khan* movie. One of these Orientals galloped over to a Russian officer in a jeep, reported something, then wheeled around and rode off at high speed, while casually raising his burp gun and firing at a passing flock of birds.

Several small groups of Russian GIs passed by on foot, looking disheveled and far from military. We exchanged greetings with some. A few stopped to share their ration of raw Army vodka and toast "Stalin, Churchill, Roosevelt!" This usually led to an invitation for us to come along with them to Berlin, an offer not always easy to refuse, but we managed to part friends every time.

By late afternoon we got word that some other *Amerikanskis* were in the area and we soon managed to track them down. They were six old kriegies who had managed to stay hidden in the hayloft despite all the firing by the German guards. They had found the town's old Nazi headquarters, strangely undamaged, where they had located and happily liberated some German food rations and even a bit of schnapps. So we quickly joined them temporarily. The SAO was Major Crandall and the group included our old chums Durgin and Holder. George was engaged in trying on some snappy-looking Hitler Youth uniforms, which he fortunately decided not to wear. They had been staying in a deserted German house and we spent the night with them undisturbed.

January 28—WIRSITZ, Poland

We spent the day watching the Russians clear out the remaining nests of Germans from this Polish crossroads town, then loot it thoroughly. Several groups of frightened Germans were uncovered as the Russians methodically checked out building after building. As far as we could tell, none were taken prisoner. The *Ruskies* simply led the captured Germans behind a building and shot them. Later, however, we did see small groups of German soldiers being marched back toward Russia, so some evidently were spared.

The Russian GIs here were a tough, rugged breed, but generally friendly and curious about Americans. Communication was difficult, since we had no common language, but some basic German. Yet we got along. Some would point to the lend-lease army trucks that drove by and identified them as *Schudabeggers* after the American label on the Studebaker vehicles. There was much cheering of Stalin and Roosevelt. Some of the Russians gave Tacy and me their Red Star insignia as a sort of momento, but happily declined our offer of U.S. Army insignia in return. One called us *capitaleest's*, but he appeared to be kidding. Many were explicit in gesturing what they planned to do with the Germans when they got to Berlin.

January 29—NACKEL, Poland

Getting out of Poland on our own posed quite a problem. As no transportation seemed to be headed east, our small group decided to split up and try to hitchhike back to Oflag 64, which presumably was now overrun by the Russians. The Soviets, we figured, would have to provide some sort of evacuation for the hospitalized kriegies, so we would maybe ride along as supercargo. So Tacy and I headed back toward Schubin.

We trudged through the snow still dragging our old sled and covered about 25 kilometers before dusk. The countryside along the road was strangely dotted this time with feet sticking up out of the snow. Those feet turned out to belong to dead German soldiers, whose good army boots had been forcibly and post-humously removed by the Russians.

By now, most of the Russians we saw were being carried forward by six-wheel *Schtudabeggers* toward the next strong point of German resistance. A great many were drinking vodka, singing and horsing around in the rear of the trucks. From time to time, one of them would fall out while rounding a curve. Once, while we watched in disbelief, a Russian GI fell out of a truck directly in the path of another and was killed instantly when the driver of the second vehicle ran over his head without attempting to avoid him. This was greeted with applause by the Russians in both trucks, probably as a tribute to precision driving.

The Polish town of Nackel was in ruins, still smoking. Most buildings seemed to be wrecked by artillery fire, not by bombing. We had seen no Soviet bombers operating with the forward troops. Nelson and I walked around the town square, cold and hungry. We were soon approached by two Poles who found we were Americans and invited us home for dinner. This turned out to be a mixed blessing, but better than nothing. Their apartment was in a partially-destroyed building with no heat, electricity, water, or functioning plumbing. It was a two-room affair, currently occupied by seven Poles. We gratefully shared their slim rations of black bread and lard. When time came to use the facilities, we were directed to the basement. There we found two dead Germans whom the Russians had been using as human latrines. We spent the night with our Polish hosts, barely fitting into the floor space available. They told us in broken German about the brutal German occupation and their even greater apprehension about what the Russians would do next. Again, they were basing their hopes on the American Army coming to their rescue. Tired as we were, I got little sleep as my portion of the apartment floor was right next to a much-used chamber pot.

January 30—SCHUBIN, Poland

We finally had to ditch our sled. Pulling it through the deep snow got too tough, so we mushed along the highway carrying our gear in improvised backpacks. After a couple of hours, we collapsed by the side of the road. The biggest tank I had ever seen clanked up beside us and stopped. We said the magic word *Amerikanski* and the tank commander welcomed us aboard. It turned out that he had seen us smoking and was out of cigarettes. So I offered him a Camel; he took the pack.

We hung onto precarious seats atop this monstrous Russian tank as it roared off at high speed. The cowboy in charge drove down the middle of the highway, scattering all other traffic to both sides until we came within sight of a town. Then he would swing out across snow-covered fields and frozen streams without slowing down appreciably. Luckily, there was no German opposition in this area, so we bounced along without stopping for 18 kilometers or so to Schubin where we jumped off. One of the tankers waved at us solemnly, then they zoomed off again.

Back at Schubin, we walked through the familiar wide-open gates of Oflag 64 and there found a terse note posted on the bulletin board by the camp SAO. A Russian truck convoy, it appears, had finally arrived the day before, packed up all the sick and wounded, and had taken off in the direction of Warsaw. We'd missed it by one day.

By then we were exhausted and my game leg was acting up, so we decided to rest up here before heading out again. The camp was a disaster, apparently looted of all supplies and equipment by the Russians or Poles—or both. One kriegy was already encamped here, Lt. Marcellus Hughes, who had wisely slipped away from the column when the German guards had briefly disappeared. He had hidden away with a Polish family much as we had. He was married to Caroline Bell Hughes, a writer on the staff of the *Washington Post* who I had known back in civilian days. Thus I was doubly happy to meet up with him at Oflag 64. We joined him and sacked out for the night in the attic library, a good out-of-the-way spot.

January 31–February 4—SCHUBIN, Poland

We were holed up here in Schubin for five days while I came down with a flu bug of some kind. Both of my roommates foraged successfully for food and drink offered by by the poor but hospitable Poles in Schubin, who had been our unseen neighbors for so long. By the time I recovered, 14 more kriegies who had escaped, of the 1,400 who marched out of camp, had joined us and we were ready to leave.

February 5—LABISZYN, Poland

One of us stopped a Russian truck that was headed back east for resupply and bribed the driver with cigarettes to take us part of the way along the road east. We all piled in and rode all day in great spirits, but without food or warmth in subzero weather. At the small Polish town of Labiszyn, we piled out. My partner Tacy and I headed automatically for the town square. Once again, a friendly Polish family took us in and we shared their dinner, a feast of borsch and something. This family lived in another small, partly-wrecked apartment, but it was not quite so crowded as the last one. We found this family even more apprehensive of the Russians and full of the latest rumors about the American Army coming to their rescue.

February 6—HOHENSALZA, Poland

Together with Holder and Durgin, Tacy and I rode out of Labiszyn in great style this morning in the back of a Polish horse-drawn haycart headed east. We stopped at a small hotel for lunch, which we got by trading some of our remaining Red Cross cigarettes. There we struck up a conversation of sorts with a handsome young Russian captain named Ivan, who fortunately was headed back to Russia on some unspecified mission. Ivan had with him a bat man who must be the world's most evil-looking soldier. We named him Boris. The captain agreed to show us how to travel in wartime Poland.

It was easy; it was a piece of cake. Boris would stand in the middle of the road and shoot off a few rounds from his burp-gun just over the head of the driver of the next oncoming army truck. The truck would screech to a stop. Ivan would get in the cab next to the driver, and the four of us with Boris would pile into the trunk of the truck. For variety, after driving for a few hours, we'd switch to another truck. By nightfall, we had reached the fair-sized city of Hohensalza.

Here Ivan took us to the best hotel in town, taken over by the Russians for the exclusive use of Soviet officers. There was no old socialist equality here. We were soon sampling the joys of their better army vodka, toasting Stalin, Roosevelt, and Churchill at length. After enough vodka was consumed, Ivan and I exchanged our uniform jackets as a gesture of allied unity. Just then a stern-visaged Russian appeared at the door and barked a few choice words. He turned out to be the political commissar attached to this army unit. Ivan sobered immediately, we reexchanged jackets, and we both vowed to mend our ways from here on. So to bed.

February 7—SOMEWHERE in Poland

We had breakfast of sorts the next morning in our army-run hotel, joined by a group of Polish officers recently escaped from German prison camps after five years behind barbed wire. It was hard to visualize what they had been through—or what was ahead for them.

Then Boris hailed a passing truck in his usual fashion, and we were off again. This vehicle had an open truckbed with 8 or 10 other passengers already seated, all civilian refugees. One was a harassed young mother, holding a small infant who was crying lustily. Boris sat next to her, scowling evilly. She tried to hush the child but couldn't. Boris scowled even more fiercely, then grabbed the baby away from its mother. The poor lady screamed, assuming that he would either throw the baby out of the truck or eat it. But Boris merely thrust the little fellow inside his army greatcoat and patted him once or twice. The baby quieted down at once and made cooing noises. We all applauded.

Today we drove all day across the snow-covered countryside spotted with wreckage of the war—shelled buildings, burned-out vehicles, unburied German corpses, and more feet sticking out of the snow. At sundown we came to another Polish town with an unpronounceable name and headed for the town square. Tacy and I once again joined a hospitable Polish family, this time with nine people sharing two crowded rooms with no heat and little food. We talked until a late hour by lamplight. They claimed firsthand knowledge that several U.S. Army divisions were already on their way to Poland, a sad misconception.

February 8—WARSAW

This was the longest day's journey yet, about 150 kilometers, made in a series of Soviet army vehicles whistled up by Boris. We traveled east through the big, ruined city of Kutno and reached Warsaw just at dusk. The city was an almost unbelievable sight, the most completely devastated metropolis imaginable. Every building of the old Polish capital appeared to be wrecked. Few walls were left standing. Only a few streets were cleared enough for use. The wreckage extended for miles, covering everything. The Russians had been here for just a month, but had done nothing but clear a path through the center of town for their army vehicles to get through.

Finding a place to spend the night was a problem, until the driver pointed to a wrecked building that had smoke coming out of the remains of a chimney. There we found steps leading down to a basement. We went down and introduced ourselves to a small group of Polish survivors of the battle of Warsaw. We offered what we could to the communal pot, then listened to their stories of the battle, told in gestures and broken German. All of them had taken part in the final uprising against the Germans and wanted to tell someone about it. Poland's General Bor, they said, gave the signal to start the insurrection as soon as Russian forces reached the far bank of the Vistula River bordering Warsaw. For some reason, however, the Soviet forces stayed across the river, so the Germans obeyed Hitler's orders and proceeded to blow up the city with dynamite and artillery, building by building and block by block.

Led by General Bor, the Polish underground fought a brave but one-sided battle, killing many of the German troops by traveling underground through the maze of city sewers and striking them from behind. In the end, the Germans succeeded in destroying their beautiful city. One member of the group that night was a young boy I'll never forget. They said he was only 12 years old, but he looked like a little old man with white hair, sunken eyes, and the expression of a veteran soldier who had seen everything. He had been a messenger and ammunition carrier during the uprising, traveling constantly through the sewers of Warsaw and operating often behind the German lines. He listened intently to the war stories but never spoke all evening.

February 9—WARSAW

We walked around the ruins of Warsaw today and were amazed at the thoroughness of the destruction. Even the trees were slashed down and destroyed. A few civilians were poking around the ruins, probably looking for their former homes. Much military traffic was now going through the city, most of it funneled across the Vistula River on a makeshift floating bridge that the Russians had thrown together. We hailed a passing *Studabegger* and crossed the bridge too, then passed through the suburb of Praha, which had less damage.

We had been advised at Schubin to look for the big refugee center said to be just outside of Warsaw. We finally found it at Rembertov, an old Polish military school a few kilometers from Praha. We weren't prepared for what we found there, however. Probably 4,000 to 5,000 war refugees of at least a dozen nationalities were milling around the old brick compound. It looked like a Polish *Dante's Inferno*. There were hundreds of homeless, ragged Polish civilians, some Serbian GIs, a contingent of British and French POWs who had escaped, lots of recently liberated Yugoslav and Polish troops, some Bulgarians, a few Norwegians, and at least one Hollander among others in the hopelessly crowded compound. Most were living like animals, sleeping in hallways, filthy, scrounging scraps of anything that might be worn or eaten. They wore mismatched pieces of old clothing, and were obviously hungry, cold, and unwell. More than a few had a leg or arm missing.

We finally located our fellow Americans, the contingent of wounded kriegies brought here from Oflag 64, led by Col. Frederick Drury, who was trying to hold things together. He said they had been here for nine days trying to get out of this pesthole, but the Russians would not promise anything or let him get in touch with the American military mission in Moscow. He asked, "Do you have any ideas?" We had none that seemed very practical at the time. So we found a place to squeeze in, with the idea of taking off on our own for Moscow if nothing developed in a day or two.

February 10—REMBERTOV, Poland

We checked into the refugee center here and enjoyed a hot shower, our first in many weeks. We also had our clothes deloused in a steam-heated oven. It was a friendly sort of arrangement. The shower was used by batches of 20 men at a time, with an old crone overseeing the operation and slapping everybody on the rear end in the process.

So-called meals were served twice a day, around noon and again around 8 p.m. They consisted of a cereal called *kasha* and glasses of what passed for hot tea. Each guest in the American sector was assigned several square feet of floor space for sleeping. All were advised to guard their belongings very closely.

Later, we walked into a nearby town to check on reports of a barter market. This local open market was set up in a few vacant lots as a sort of bazaar where refugees could swap their spare possessions for something else or sell them for Polish *zloties*. A quick check indicated that a *zloty* was worth about 20 cents American. But supply and demand ruled here too. You could get 70 *zloties*, worth maybe $14, for a pack of American cigarettes, while a small piece of black bread would cost 50 *zloties*, a tasteless sugarless pastry 30 *zloties*, a piece of mystery meat (widely assumed to be dog or dead German) 150 *zloties* a pound, or a used wristwatch for around 800 *zloties*. Ragged refuges were trading all sorts of things, including nails, knives, caps, coats, battered pans, and forks for any kind of food.

We then visited the Rembertov hospital where the more seriously wounded kriegies were bedded down. All the doctors were Russians women, bustling, efficient types. The facilities were primitive and medication apparently scarce.

"Boomer" Holder was there, suffering with some undiagnosed ailment aggravated by the cold. Wright Bryan, a civilian war correspondent who wound up at Oflag 64 with a wounded leg, was there too, immobile but in good spirits. He wrote for *The Atlanta Journal*, was the first correspondent to broadcast from the D-Day landings, and helped me considerably with *The Item*. My leg, fortunately, was better and so I was not tempted to try out the Soviet medical facilities.

February 11—RENBERTOV

A few American enlisted men arrived here today. They are supposed to be the advance party for up to 1,000 noncommissioned officers (NCOs) whose prison camp in southern Poland was overrun before the Germans could move them out. We hope the rest of them make it; this bunch looks pretty hungry.

With more civilian refugees showing up every day, this place is looking more like a train terminal operating around the clock. Our two daily meals got served later and later, today at 3 p.m. and midnight, but boasting soup, barley and tea. Almost everyone now had a case of galloping dysentery. We see a lot of the latrines; they consist of a room with standard men's urinals on one side and half a dozen holes in the floor on the other. The latrines are all used by both sexes, simultaneously and continually, including the urinals, which are used by the ladies with much dexterity.

February 12–19—REMBERTOV

The Russian commander here now promises us a special shipment of food, warm clothing, medicines, and railroad transportation directly to Moscow. But nothing has arrived and we are still here. Col. Drury managed to get off a wire to the U.S. Embassy in Moscow, so we'll wait here a bit longer to see what happens. There are now 240 U.S. officers and 480 enlisted men here, with no more expected. The latest batch to arrive were kriegies from Oflag 64, who were on the long march but were in such bad physical shape that the Germans turned them loose about 40 kilometers from Stettin. From there, they managed to hitch rides to Bromberg, then got aboard a freight train bound for Warsaw. They report undergoing some shelling when they were overrun by the Russian army, but luckily they suffered no casualties.

There was only one meal today, and that one almost inedible. There is no heat and not enough floor space left to sleep on, so we alternate in sitting up. The refugees keep coming by truck and boxcars and on foot. Many of them are piti-ful sights—old women carrying sick husbands, people riding atop locomotive engines, kids balancing themselves on couplings between crowded freight cars, people dead on their feet. It's a fantastic, unbelievable sight and we are anxious to leave one way or the other.

Meanwhile, without our knowledge, we Americans at Rembertov had caused a diplomatic blowup of sorts between Washington and Moscow. As it turned out later, here is what happened:

Maj. Gen. John R. Deane, chief of the U.S. Military Mission in Moscow, had gone to great lengths to provide for the anticipated influx of Americans across Poland.[1] As early as June 11, 1944, a few days after the allied invasion of Normandy, he had approached the Red Army General Staff in Moscow with a list of U.S. and British prisoner of war camps known to be in the path of the Russian advance. He asked that the Russians let U.S. forces send in supplies and help evacuate any escapees or liberated prisoners. There was no reply. Then on August 30, Averill Harriman, our ambassador to Moscow, sent a letter prepared by General Deane to V. M. Molotov, foreign minister of the USSR, suggesting that the two countries set up some arrangements for the prompt return of each other's liberated prisoners. There was no reply to either of these letters for several months, although both Harriman and Deane kept after their Kremlin contacts.

Then General Deane set up a board of officers to prepare a workable plan for handling any kriegies who might get free in Poland. This group went allout in its preparation and apparently did a thorough job of it. A stockpile of medical supplies, new clothing, and even luxury items like candy and tobacco, was assembled in England for the use of freed POWs. The board arranged for the Persian Gulf Command to set aside a reserve for quick delivery of these supplies by air to any points that Deane would designate in Poland or Russia.

---

[1]John R. Deane. *The Strange Alliance*. The Viking Press. New York.

Special hospital accommodations were set aside at the U.S. air base inside Russia at Poltava where American planes were being ferried into Russia. Plans were then made to fly all the seriously ill from Poland to Poltava for medical attention and evacuation.

In Moscow, General Deane also arranged to have a group of special qualified U.S. officers and NCOs sent from Britain to Russia to travel around inside Soviet-overrun territory and make contact with any American military men they might find. Each of these Americans would speak fluent Russian and adequate Polish.

Then in December 1944, as the Russians took Warsaw and started their big offensive across northern Poland, Ambassador Harriman wrote Molotov again and asked for quick development of plans to provide for our POWs. Two senior Russian officers, Lt. Gen. K.D. Golubev and Maj. Gen. Slavin—finally met with General Deane on January 19, just two days before we marched out of Oflag 64. They worked out a formal agreement for handling repatriation problems on both sides, including plans for the freed American prisoners. This agreement was a good one, Deane said, covering the business of sending supplies and training people to contact liberated Americans and get them out quickly. It was signed in Moscow, then signed again at the Yalta conference between President Roosevelt and Stalin a few weeks later in February.

But as Deane said later, "It turned out to be just another piece of paper." The Russians refused to allow the American mission to send any of the accumulated supplies to the liberated camps or to Rembertov, which had been designated as the assembly point for all freed Americans. They also flatly banned any of the talented, Russian-speaking U.S. officers who had been assembled for that purpose from going into Poland to contact the Americans at Rembertov or anywhere else. Nor would they permit General Deane to send his big transport planes into Poland to pick up the growing group of ex-POWs there.

All this, Deane says, came from the Kremlin itself—a top policy decision by the Soviet government. So then the White House got into the act. On two occasions, President Roosevelt attempted to help with personal appeals to Stalin but these attempts produced no noticeable results either.

Ambassador Harriman, in the middle of all this, became "relentless in his pressure on the Soviet Foreign Office," as General Deane reports it. The U.S. Army Air Force was told to make eight four-engine transports available to Deane's military mission in Moscow. They did, but the planes were never allowed in to Russia for this purpose. The U.S. Navy, in turn, was ordered to send a special shipload of supplies from Italy to Odessa to provide medicines, clothing and food for the freed prisoners in case they were able to reach that Russian port. Even so, it was late in February before the Russians made any concessions at all, when they finally agreed to provide enough boxcars to transport the growing group of Americans out of Rembertov down to Odessa.

Now to get back to the diary—

February 19—REMBERTOV

The good news finally arrived tonight. We're to leave for Russia in three days by train for some port. The destination isn't clear yet, but with the Baltic now iced in, we're guessing at a port on the Black Sea.

Someone must have gotten through to the Russians. Along with the promise of some transport out of here, Marshal Zhukov has sent the American contingent here an unbelievable gift of captured German stores: some chocolate, a barrel of wine, a few food rations, cigarettes, and even a few cigars. We are gorging ourselves.

Before the good word arrived, Nelson Tacy got itchy and took off on his own to hitchhike south, aiming for Lublin, now the temporary capital of a communist government of Poland. I bowed out. A few other kriegies have tried this route, while at least three or four optimists have headed out for Moscow. No word from any of them yet.

February 20–23—REMBERTOV

Our train to take us across Russia turns out to be a bunch of unheated boxcars headed for Odessa, but that beats walking. There are bunks in the boxcars with accommodations for about 220 U.S. officers and 600 GIs, plus about 400 British. The plan is to assign 30 men to each boxcar. This arrangement seems to be standard Russian army transport with double-plank platforms for bunks furnished with straw mattresses, an issue of Russian army blankets, a wood-burning stove for each car, and a couple of water pails. Food and fuel may or may not be provided.

So we prepared for a long, slow trip across the steppes of Russia, by bartering everything we could spare at the local bazaar. I sold my sweater, the fountain pen I had used for putting out *The Daily Bulletin*, some stubby pencils, and other odds and ends. With all those *zloties*, I stocked up on Polish black bread, which lasts forever.

Right on schedule, we marched out to the Rembertov railroad yard at 9 a.m., climbed aboard our assigned boxcars, and then waited all day while watching hefty Russian army women direct traffic and load timber onto the wood-burning locomotives. We spent the night in the same Rembertov marshaling yard, bedded down in our own cozy boxcar.

February 24—EN ROUTE, in Poland

We're off at last. Our Russian freight train pulled out sometime during the night and reached Sydice, about 90 kilometers east of Warsaw, by 9 a.m. Here, much to our surprise, the Russians provided us with some cabbage soup. Just before we pulled out again, we were greeted by a long-bearded civilian con man who was looking to buy American watches. I dickered with him at length over my old $1 Ingersoll, which would only run for about 10 minutes at a time. (I had asked my family to send me the cheapest possible watch so that it wouldn't be confiscated by the Germans.) Then, just as the train started up, I wound the watch up and let him have it for a handful of *zloties*. So now we had some cash on hand for trading en route.

Our train moved slowly along the wide-gauge tracks and burned only wood, so we had to stop frequently to take on fuel and water. These stops gave the passengers time for many half-hour bartering sessions at the towns where we stopped. Despite the cold, we left the side door to our boxcar open to enjoy the snow-covered plains of Poland.

February 25—EN ROUTE, in Russia

As the snow began to fall heavily, we crossed the Bug River into Russia early this morning. The border appears to be unmarked. It was considerably west of the old, prewar border. The first stop in Russia was at Brest-Litovsk.

From here our Soviet troop train headed south for the long, 1,500-mile trek across the Russian steppes, now covered with about three feet of snow and flat as the plains of the American Midwest. By nightfall, we reached the town of Kowel and, for some reason, we laid over there for the night.

The next day, we passed a whole trainload of German prisoners headed north. They did not look happy, and they were packed in tightly. We figured there were at least 90 men to the boxcar. Their doors were locked shut, of course, but barred windows were open and filled with sad, drawn faces.

February 26—EN ROUTE

Heavy snow obscured much of the Russian steppes now as we moved south. Life in an open box car was cold but bearable, we found. A Russian soldier was traveling with us to show us the ropes: how to keep a wood fire going in the boxcar stove, how to keep warm by burrowing in the straw, and where to sit to avoid the wintry blasts and enjoy the view. The train stopped frequently, which was handy for answering the calls of nature and for quick barter operations at the open markets at every stop along the way. I traded my German cigars for some almost-white bread at one stop, a great bargain, I thought. Once or twice a day, a sort of soup was served to all comers outside the kitchen car. You just brought your own utensils. The towns all appeared badly damaged by artillery fire. Half a dozen of our 30 kriegies were sick by now with some kind of flu bug, but not me.

February 27—EN ROUTE

We covered probably 200 miles today, across flat Russian snow-covered terrain spotted with small clusters of pine trees and occasional settlements or single, isolated farmhouses that all showed signs of war damage. Many of the houses were adobe style with thatched roofs. The weather was very cold, likely below zero, so we exercised a lot during the frequent stops.

There were two meals today, featuring the ubiquitous Russian *kasha* with black bread and tea. We passed several other troop trains like ours, often manned by women or young boys. Brawny females would heave chunks of wood, or shovel something that looked like coal dust compressed with oil, into the fireboxes of each train. There seemed to be no passenger trains; everything moved by boxcar or flatcar.

February 28—EN ROUTE

We were now traveling down through the Ukraine. Nearly all the villages and railroad depots were in ruins from the fierce battles last year in this area. It was getting warmer, so I started selling more pieces of clothing. We were dealing here in Russian *rubles,* at highly inflated prices. With a supposed exchange rate of 5 *rubles* for $1, eggs were selling for $1 apiece, buns for $2 each, a pair of socks for $40, and a pair of army blankets for $200.

Most of our boxcar bunch were down now with some respiratory ailment, but the end was in sight. We halted tonight just 10 miles from Odessa.

March 1—ODESSA, Russia

We finally reached this big Black Sea port early this morning. The city is in bad shape under its cover of snow. The railroad station was about leveled by shelling, and most other major buildings were damaged to some extent. There were no automobiles in sight, only army trucks and jeeps. But the sun was shining and the civilians looked better than any we had seen for a long time. Some of the women even wore lipstick, a highly unusual sight for us. Our little group of Americans was met by a sort of military band, which attempted to play "Roll Out the Barrel" over and over. We hiked and hobbled for several miles through the city of Odessa. It was a good feeling.

Then our group of Americans was moved into an imposing building labeled in Russian, "Polygon No. 2," reported to be the former Italian consulate. It was located in a little park surrounded by an iron fence. Unfortunately, there was no heat, lights, or water. The Russians quickly stationed guards around the place to see that no Americans could climb over the fence and go into town.

March 2–6—ODESSA

Our frustrations in dealing with the Russians grew rapidly. We were unable to get out of the compound to barter for food, which we now needed badly. Meals were served twice a day, but consisted solely of nearly inedible fish heads and tea. The cold was penetrating, and there was no way to get fuel for the stoves. Both of my traveling friends, Holder and Durgin, were down with the grippe or something. Diarrhea had returned full force, as well. We couldn't find out what the Russians had in mind for us, or when and how we might leave.

To our great surprise, a young American major who speaks fluent Russian showed up one day, sent by the U.S. military mission in Moscow. His name was Paul Hill. He had learned his Russian at New York University and said he was here unofficially and semilegally. He reported that much pressure was being put on the Soviets in Moscow and Washington to let the U.S. Army fly in supplies for us and then to fly us out of this place. But, for some reason, the Russians wouldn't agree. They seemed to be holding things up deliberately. So there was no telling when we might get out of here.

There was one good development. My escape buddy, Nelson Tacy, finally showed up. He said that he got to Lublin and things were just as bad there. He and a few other kriegies hopped a train and headed here. Now we started to plan how we might bust out of the consulate and hop aboard a ship going somewhere. The question was how.

At this point, Ambassador Harriman was seeing Andrei Vyshinsky, the Soviet deputy foreign minister, in an effort to get some action. When none was forthcoming, he radioed President Roosevelt. The President then sent a message to Stalin, whom he had seen a month before at Yalta, asking him to let General Deane send his contact officers and supplies to the Americans who were now inside Russia. Stalin replied a few days later, saying that the situation was well in hand and that all this would not be necessary. He concluded his message by saying that the Americans were being well cared for in Soviet camps in contrast to the treatment being afforded Soviet former prisoners of war then in American camps in Europe, who were housed with German prisoners and suffering unjust treatment.

This exchange apparently marked the official end of the wartime honeymoon between Russia and the United States. From here on, Stalin, Molotov, and other Soviet officials poured forth a continuous stream of accusations about the terrible treatment Soviet citizens were receiving at the hands of liberating U.S. forces in Europe. In nearly all cases, General Eisenhower's staff reported that these accusations proved to be totally false. Later, Soviet representatives at U.S. field headquarters in Europe admitted the accusations were unfounded.

For various reasons, it seemed that Moscow was anxious to get the many thousands of liberated Russian prisoners back into the Soviet Union quickly. It became apparent, too, that the Kremlin wanted to hold onto the Americans then in Russia as long as possible, as pawns in this endeavor.[2]

To return again to the diary—

March 7—ODESSA

Suddenly, early this morning, the Russians relented. At long last, we marched out of Polygon 2 through the potholed streets of Odessa to the half-wrecked dock area facing the Black Sea. In the harbor, to our astonishment, were three American freighters—the first to dock here in 22 years, we're told. We weren't allowed to board them for a ride home, unfortunately, and the crew was not permitted ashore. But we shouted back and forth and got caught up on some news of the war and the home front. The civilian sailors told us, laughingly, that they were all a bunch of draft-dodgers.

Our exodus, instead, was to be aboard a British freighter, the *Moreton Bay*, which had just arrived with a cargo of lend-lease supplies and several hundred newly liberated Russian prisoners of war. The returning Russians seemed to be unduly apprehensive about coming home; many had to be dragged out of the hold where they had hidden in out-of-the-way crannies. We replaced them with a lot more enthusiasm. Close to 2,000 British and American ex-POWs were all of us anxious to get the hell out of Russia as soon as possible.

In time everybody was fitted in. The few staterooms were assigned to our field-grade officers and we juniors were provided with hammocks below deck. There was a lounge of sorts and even a bar, but no liquor. Best of all, there was the ship's dining room where we were soon served the best meal of my life. The menu included real coffee, genuine white bread, edible soup, delicious canned roast beef, elegant mashed potatoes, and a superb junket. We cast off late in the day, headed in the general direction of Turkey.

---

[2]Ibid.

March 8–13—AT SEA

Although our ship was crowded, this trip has been a memorable—across the Black Sea and through the Bosphorus with an overnight anchorage overlooking Istanbul and its minarets, turned-on street lights, working streetcars, civilian auto traffic, and distant mosques. We then proceeded through the Dardanelles and along the Mediterranean coast to Egypt's Port Said at the entrance to the Suez Canal.

March 14–16—PORT SAID, Egypt

We landed here at a well-stocked U.S. Army transient camp and spent three days getting our group of skinny, disreputable kriegies back into decent shape. We scrubbed up, got haircuts, exchanged our decrepit old uniforms for good new ones, got half a dozen shots and a lot of medication, sent cables to wives, and cautiously tried a British beverage called whiskey. I found that I was down to 127 pounds in weight, about 50 pounds under normal, and tried to make it up by eating around the clock. We also started to thaw out and even did a bit of sightseeing. With a small salary advance, I managed to buy a new watch that worked.

March 17–19—AT SEA

We sailed from Port Said aboard another British ship, the *TSS Samaria,* also crowded but blessed with good food and fair accommodations, bound for Naples. There followed three days of beautiful weather with a smooth sea and apparently no need for convoying.

March 20–29—NAPLES, Italy

Our ship docked at Naples and we were bused out to the Terme Hotel, a former health resort some eight miles out of town. It was well equipped with hospital facilities, a hot sulfur spring, some palm trees, comfortable beds, and a fine dining room.

There everybody got more shots, a thorough physical exam, a lot of forms to fill out, and a sightseeing tour of Naples. Only the waterfront seemed to show any war damage, but the city was badly run down. I located Wright Bryan at the U.S. Army Hospital in town, where his leg was slowly healing. I also saw Ed Nixon of the Associated Press at the Naples office of *Stars and Stripes.* One day

Durgin, Holder and I took a train out to see the ruins of Pompeii, then had dinner at the 32nd Station Hospital officers' club. Somewhere along the line, I was presented with a Purple Heart for a minor leg wound incurred, it seemed, at least 110 years ago.

March 30–April 9—AT SEA

From Naples, we boarded an American troop ship, the *USS Mariposa, a* former Matson Line cruise ship, and set out for home across the Mediterranean and the Atlantic. We spent the next 10 days luxuriating in a nine-man stateroom, eating two great meals a day, and enjoying a smooth crossing.

By the time we landed at Boston, we had pretty much agreed on one lesson learned from our recent travels: the Russians are great fighters but they think and act very differently than we do in wartime. We had better understand that difference well if we ever have to tangle with them. Hopefully we never will.

The Long Cold March

11 When the camp was evacuated in January 1945, the tough part had just begun for most of the American prisoners. Leaving behind only 86 of the badly wounded officers, 1,471 kriegies were marched out through the gates for a 345-mile trek into Germany. It took 45 days on foot, trudging through deep snow with inadequate rations and medical supplies, to their destination of Brandenburg.

Because I was fortunate enough to escape on the third night out, I cannot give a first-hand account of that long, grueling march. But an old kriegy friend, Dr. Peter C. Graffagnino, walked the distance and later reported the experience in a medical newsletter that he contributed to regularly. Graf was one of those rare doctors who likes to write and writes well. Here is his report on what the long march was like:

As we marched out of the prisoner of war camp in Poland in the sub-zero cold of late January 1945, we knew little of our destination or what the Germans planned for us. The march had been organized hurriedly by our German captors in an attempt to evacuate the camp before the rapidly advancing Russians could overrun it. *Oberst* Schneider, the portly, officious commandant of the German garrison, and his executive officer, *Hauptman* Menner, a kindly and apologetic Viennese, bustled impatiently around the camp's barbed-wire gates until the last of the departing prisoners had cleared. Then they sped off in their small, battered car, scooting and skidding past the marchers to reach the head of the column. The only other transportation available, a decrepit wood-burning truck that followed, carrying platform supplies and mess equipment on its open back, along with some grumbling guards to serve as relief relays for those who marched beside us.

The countryside through which we were moving was blanketed under deep snow. Above a steely hoarfrost haze, the skies were bright and the air was quiet and still. We were bundled in clothing with our heads and faces swathed in makeshift hoods of blankets, scarves, and sweaters, but the cold was still penetrating and bone-chilling. The condensing vapor of our breathing crusted in fine, icy crystals on our lashes and eyebrows and along the edges of of the woolen coverings over our mouths and noses. There was no way to crowd more than a few layers of socks into a pair of GI shoes, and it was our feet that suffered most.

In contrast to the unhappy armed guards who slugged along beside us, we were in high spirits. Most of us were burdened under packs and blanket rolls with an accumulated hoard of canned and packaged food that we had squirreled away over the months from Red Cross parcels for just such an emergency. On the first day of marching, however, the discomforts of our staggering loads and chilled bodies were counteracted by the excitement of being out from behind the barbed wire and on the open road again. The terrain was new, and our interest in the changing scenery was keyed to a fever pitch of alertness by constant speculation about opportunities to take off on our own and escape.

We headed south originally in the general direction of Posnan, a rail center about 65 miles away, but after covering about six miles, we found our direction abruptly changed to west and again after a short time to north. *Oberst* Schneider, scouting ahead in his car, had learned that the Russians had cut across below us.

For the next seven days, we marched, covering ten miles to eighteen miles a day. There was no letup in the cold, but the weather remained favorable with only an occasional light snowfall. We traveled mainly on the secondary rural roads, over a zigzag route, northward and westward, our direction changing from day to day according to the whim of *Oberst* Schneider and the reports he received on his scouting excursions ahead of the column. It was evident that the whole area was in a state of confusion. At times, particularly on the larger highways, we encountered streams of civilian refugees moving in the same direction as we were, while at other times they passed us in the opposite direction.

These photos of the long, cold march from Oflag 64 for 345 miles back into Germany were taken by an anonymous prisoner somewhere along the line. They came to light at a reunion some time after the war and are considered to be authentic.

Znin, Wyrzysk, Kenia, Szamocin, Schneidemuhl, Krojanke, Zlotow—we moved through all these towns, villages, and farm settlements, many of them almost completely deserted and nearly all with strange, tongue-twisting Polish names. We slept outdoors in straw piled on the snow, in barns, abandoned farmhouses, warehouses, meeting halls, cattle pens, deserted barracks, whatever shelter was available when night came. We ate up our hoarded supplies of personal food, our daily ration of sour black bread ("goon" bread, to the POWs), and the occasional tinned beef issued to us by the Germans. At the end of a day's march, there was sometimes a dipperful of watery stew, compounded from vegetables, barley, and horse meat, doled out by the Germans into whatever containers we had.

As the days passed, we marched more grimly and determinedly. The enthusiasm and expectation of the first days on the road had dulled and disappeared in our fight against constant cold, fatigue and hunger. Each morning, as we were reassembled and moved on, a group of 50 to 100 prisoners was left behind. Old infirmatives and war wounds, sickness, and plain exhaustion took its toll on men already undernourished and unaccustomed to prolonged exertion after months or years of prison inactivity. By far the greatest incapacitating ailment was the recurrence of old trench foot and frostbite. The Germans allowed one or two of the doctors (more than two dozen of us had started with the column) to remain with each group left behind.

All during the march we walked with Arthur Mallory, my double-decker bunkmate for the last five months at Schubin. Mallory, a Citadel graduate, had been a company commander in another regiment of our own 45th Division and had been captured in the same convulsive battle on the Anzio beachhead almost a year before. Every night, whether huddled together in the straw piles, burrowed into a haystack, or sheltered in some barn, we argued the merits of leaving the column, joining a sick group, or hiding out. But, by day, we were always marching again. There was safety in numbers. There was compulsion too. Even though our hands were blue and numb, our feet frostbitten, and our limbs exhausted, we were determined to walk as long as others were walking.

There was also a medical conscience that would not let us abandon the men and the two or three doctors who still marched with the column. Although there was nothing we could do medically for the sick ones, we were conscious that the continued presence of even one sorry, unmilitary pill-peddler somehow boosted the morale of the marchers.

Once at nightfall we were herded into the barns and outbuildings of a large estate at Charlottenberg. The manor house, a spired and turreted mansion with gingerbread gables and piazzas, rested in an icy wonderland of snow and crystalline trees, shimmering in cold, blue moonlight, looking like a fantasy from an Anderson fairy tale. With Mallory, I lined up for chow, the inevitable thick barley soup that was being measured out from a makeshift kitchen under the porte cochere of the main house. Somehow the two of us slipped unnoticed into the house itself. We ate our porridge in an elegant music room, lavishly furnished in Victorian style, and after eating, we set out to explore some of the ground floor rooms. In the library we came unexpectedly upon a group of unfamiliar German officers busy over maps. We identified ourselves and, on the pretext of some official nature, requested permission to look through the house for drugs and medicines. Whether it was our boldness or the Germans' preoccupation with their own worsening predicament, we were allowed to go on.

By the ninth day, we had covered over 100 miles and fewer than 800 of us were still marching. The skies were leaden, the winds biting, and as we marched the snow flurries increased. By mid afternoon we were struggling forward against a howling blizzard. The cold was almost paralyzing. The countryside was flat and open, offering no protection against the blowing, driving snow. For miles there was nothing behind us that we could return to and, as far as we knew, no hope of shelter ahead. We kept moving slowly and just as our endurance was at its end, we came upon an unnamed hamlet, a group of four or five deserted farm cottages lined along each side of the road. We stumbled into this unexpected haven, overcome with exhaustion and relief.

We were divided into groups and billeted in the houses. In a short time we had a fire going in the open hearth and had foraged and found enough stored vegetables and potatoes to concoct a hot mush. After eating, we stretched out on the bare earthen floor in front of the fire and slept. The blizzard raged on outside and finally subsided during the night, but none of us knew it. We slept a sleep of the dead. It was the most comfortable night we had passed since starting the march.

When we awakened in the morning there was none of the usual noise and rustle of previous mornings, no clatter of hobnailed boots, no prodding with gun-butts, no shouts of *Raus* or *Schnell*!! The snow had stopped and as we poked about, cautiously at first and then with more boldness, we discovered that our

German guards were gone. During the night, *Oberst* Schneider and his weary, dispirited men had pulled out and deserted us. We were free.

We spent the day organizing and planning. Food parties discovered and rounded up some chickens and pigs. Kitchen details went into action and prepared a feast. With a day of welcome rest, food and warmth, our fatigue disappeared and our enthusiasm returned. Unfortunately there was no place to go. We were isolated in a vast expanse of winter wasteland in the middle of nowhere. The weather was colder than before, with a temperature almost 30 degrees below zero. We reasoned that since the Germans had deserted us, the Russians must be close by. Therefore, our best bet was to remain where we were and wait to be found. So we stayed.

With nighttime came the sound of motors and we hurried out of the houses. Our Russian vocabulary was limited to two words, *tovarich* and *vodka*, and we were eager to use them. Our jubilation was short-lived, however; the Germans had come back. *Oberst* Schneider had run afoul of a motorized SS Latvian unit and had been made to return and take us back into custody. He was frightened and almost apologetic. With him this time were fresh troops and an SS major who did not smile. We remained in the houses again that night, but once again as prisoners.

The brief taste of freedom, however, had stirred the prisoners. Some were rebellious and unruly, and a few skirmishes broke out between these men and the guards. Although there were enough of us in each house to overpower the few armed Germans who guarded us, caution prevailed again. The end seemed too near. We had come too far and had survived too long to risk challenging the Germans. There were some impulsive ones and some bitter ones, half-crazed with disappointment, who resisted. From this house or that one, an occasional pistol shot or the rattle of an automatic weapon kept us awake most of the night. We left a handful of wounded and three or four dead when we marched away in the morning.

When the marching group, with some aid from a shuttling truck, reached Stettin some days later, we were quartered in marine barracks on the shore of the Dammacher Sea. Here we were given a day or two of rest; even so, when it was time to resume the march, there were almost 150 men who could not continue. Along with Lt. Col. David Gold, we were the last two doctors left with the group. He assigned me to remain with the 150 whom the Germans had agreed to move by rail. The rest marched on and Col. Gold marched with them.

The next day we were taken by truck to the railyards and loaded into two cars, a slatted boxcar made for cattle and an open coal car with a tarpaulin covering. The accommodations were crowded and not very luxurious, but it was better than walking. We were headed for Berlin. Although Stettin is less than 100 miles north of the capital, it took us four days to reach the railyards there. The German rail system was having its problems at that time. We marveled then, and have since that time, at the obstinacy and unreasoning discipline of the German mentality concerning itself with moving two carloads of prisoners while its homeland was disintegrating all around it.

In the Berlin railyards, our two railcars sat out three days and nights, back in the almost forgotten sounds of war. There were day bombings and night bombings. Some of the nighttime fireworks were spectacular displays. Miraculously there were no hits on near-misses in the vicinity of our sidetrack. Then one day, we were moving again.

Our final destination was Stalag VIII C, the large central collecting camp at Luckenwalde, about 40 miles southeast of Berlin. It was there that the Germans were funneling all the prisoners evacuated from the many camps in eastern Germany. Almost four weeks later, Col. Gold and the battered remnants of the original walking column arrived, still on foot. And it was there where we sat and waited for the war in Europe to end.

An official report, prepared later in 1945 by the Military Intelligence Service of the War Department, tells what happened next:

There had been continuous trouble in providing transportation for the sick. No effort was made to provide proper places for sick call. The ration provided on the march was inadequate. The German ration office stated that they were receiving the same ration as the German guard company, but this was not true. The average ration for the day was one bowl of turnip soup, a few potatoes, a cup of ersatz coffee or mint tea, and half a slice of brown bread. The only supplement to this diet was an occasional barter with the farmers along the way who wanted cigarettes, soap, fountain pens, etc., until finally 500 Red Cross parcels were obtained on February 17, 1945. These parcels had to be shared by

Half a century later, *Item* artist Jim Bickers vividly remembered the bitter cold march back to Germany in this sketch.

1,023 men. Only 423 officers and 67 enlisted men completed the trek to Oflag 13B, arriving in a state of exhaustion.

On March 27, Col. Goode was notified that camp 13B would be evacuated that afternoon at 1600 hours. At 1300, American tanks appeared, and after a brief consultation, the Germans agreed to surrender the camp immediately. Three of the staff officers and one German officer were selected to carry the white flag of surrender to the American tank column. As they marched out of the gate, an SS private shot Lt. Col. John K Waters, seriously wounding him. Immediately the tanks started firing and after a few minutes, the camp was in the hands of the Americans. However, the spearhead was not prepared to transport so many officers, and it was impossible to remain there and defend the area. Many of the men climbed on the tanks and attempted to get back to the (American) lines that night, but roadblocks and mines hampered their progress.

The following two days saw nearly all of the men returned to the camp under German guard. Meanwhile, the Germans had returned to evacuate the remaining prisoners to southern Germany. About 500 men were sent to Nurenberg by train. Two days later, the remaining men were marched to Stalag 7A in Moosburg. This trip was approximately 90 miles. It required 15 days to march, however, because of the weakened condition of the men and the constant bombing by the Allied air forces of stations along the way. Many men escaped during this march in the confusion. Upon their arrival at Stalag 7A, Col. Goode organized the camp of 30,000 POWs for their final rescue, which occurred on April 29, 1945.

Epilogue

Looking back more than half a century later, it is clear that the American prisoners bore up remarkably well through a nightmare of short rations and some major discomforts, harassments, and intermittent boredom. A few are still hospitalized. But nearly all found ways of coping.

How well these American POWs coped made me want to look for the source of their strength. It may be basically the American character, but I suspect that it was also something that made that generation of young men especially rugged and resourceful. The evidence points to the Great Depression, which forced those who grew up in the 1930s to cope with tribulations and try harder to help themselves and each other.

When I got back to the United States in April 1945, the war was nearly over. I received three months' leave, which I spent getting reacquainted with Tracy and my family after a second honeymoon at the Ben Franklin Hotel in Philadelphia. Then I was assigned, still as a lieutenant, to Fort McNair in Washington as a press officer for the infantry for the final few weeks of the war. With the stern advice from my wife, who didn't like three-year separations, I resigned from the Army and elected not to keep a reserve commission after the war. The next week I returned to journalism and spent nearly 40 good years with the newsmagazine, *U.S. News & World Report,* retiring with the title of Senior Editor. My first move in retirement was to write a book about our old benefactor, Henry Soederberg.

Looking back now, I ask myself how I view those years spent as a prisoner of war and an escapee, out through wartime Poland and Russia? People often ask me about it. The answer, I suppose, is that it was an experience that I would never want to repeat, but one that was definitely a high point in my life and one that I am glad I experienced. It also made me proud to be an American soldier after the way nearly all of them coped as prisoners of the Nazi Germans.

Since the war, friendships begun during those traumatic years remained and blossomed. The careers of former *Oflagites* have been truly impressive. All of those who stayed in the Army reached a rank of at least lieutenant colonel and half a dozen or more made general. Johnny Waters wound up with four stars and became commanding general of all Army forces in the Pacific during the Vietnam war. The rest made their mark in many civilian fields. They have been on White House staffs, sat on boards of large corporations, been editors of major daily newspapers, produced Broadway shows, become engineers of great renown, owned and operated radio stations, edited magazines, written books, and excelled in many other fields.

Reunions of former kriegies began a few years after the war and became a regular event every two years thereafter. These reunions have been sponsored by volunteers who would organize a three- or four-day weekend in places like New York, Washington, Las Vegas, San Diego, Miami, Louisville, and the like. Attendance at these reunions quickly grew to between 100 and 200, sometimes more as additional ex-kriegies heard about the reunions. After the ex-*Oflagites* began to die off in large numbers, their widows and sons would attend, keeping the numbers up.

The sparkplug of this movement for many years was former Lt. John Slack, who early on started a monthly newsletter telling where people were, what they were doing, and when and where the next planned reunion was to be held. After John did this stint for nearly 50 years as an adjunct to his printing business, it was taken over by Lt. Col. Herb Garris, and more recently by Bob Thompson. The reunions, meanwhile, were stepped up to once every year. The odd thing about this group was that there has never been a formal organization. No officers were elected, no dues collected, no voting done on where the next reunion would be held except at the brief "business meetings" at each one with the current host acting as chairman.

For the 50th anniversary of Oflag 64's demise, the surviving kriegies attended an especially elaborate reunion hosted by Bill Cory in Louisville, Kentucky, with much entertainment, boatrides, speeches, a banquet and even a speech by Henry Soederberg. They also put out a big, 240-page anniversary book, of which I served as editor, including personal accounts of life at Oflag 64, facsimiles of all 15 issues of the *Oflag Item*, a chapter of escape secrets by Col. Jack Van Vliet, all the theater programs, and memorabilia of all kinds. Each of the "active" ex-kriegies bought an average of 3 to 5 copies of the book at $50 a copy. We almost, but not quite, made expenses on that one.

Henry came to America often after the war. He first made a long lecture tour of the country for the YMCA, then returned again as a member of the Swedish foreign service. After that, he spent several decades with Scandinavian Airlines, coming to America about once a year and winding up as vice president in charge of overseas planning. Henry always looked up friends from Oflag 64 across the country. He soon began to attend our biannual and later annual reunions, speaking at most of them and being the featured speaker at one or two. While with Scandinavian Airlines, he arranged trips for groups of kriegies to return to visit the old camp in 1971, 1985 and 1990, with side trips to places like Warsaw, Moscow, Stockholm, Copenhagen, Vienna, St. Petersburg and Paris. Henry and his charming wife, Claire, became good friends of my wife and me over the years, visiting each others' homes and going on several vacation trips together.

At one recent reunion, Henry was presented with a plaque making him an "Honorary Kriegy, with all the Rights and Privileges Adherent Thereto." He was amused, but touched. The plaque now resides with most of his wartime memorabilia in the "Soederberg Room" of the POW section of the Air Force Academy in Colorado Springs. I also wrote a book based on Henry's wartime diaries, called *The Welcome Swede*. Henry died just a month after attending his last Oflag 64 reunion at Newport, Rhode Island, with his wife in September 1997.

The brave Dudziak family in Poland, who hid me out until the Russians arrived also became good friends after the war and remained so for four generations! Soon after hostilities ended in Europe, Tracy and I began sending CARE packages of food to the Dudziaks and later took them gifts of clothing and other things when we visited Poland on the "Kriegy Safari" of 1971. Writing was a

Henry Soederberg (on the right) and the author at Henry's home in Stockholm during a visit in 1990.

problem because of differences in languages, but we both wrote often. First I got the Polish embassy in Washington to translate my letters to them, but this had its drawbacks, so I tried writing in my fractured German. Then I simply wrote in English and the Dudziaks had my letters translated by an English-speaking Pole who also translated their letters into basic but understandable English.

The youngest boy, Jan Dudziak, was named the middleman and we corresponded for years as he grew up. Jan became a teacher and actually taught at the boys' school on the campus of what had been Oflag 64. Then both father and mother Dudziak died. We received proper photographs of them individually in their coffins.

In time, Jan and his wife produced a talented young boy, who was directed to learn correct English in order to be the go-between with the Diggs family in Washington. He did, too. When he became 17, we brought young Darek Dudziak over for a visit. He flew to New York, where our daughter Peggy showed him the city. Then came down to Washington to meet us. We entertained him for a few days and sent him off for a month-long flying trip around the country, staying mostly with old kriegy friends of mine—the Howard Holders in Atlanta, Georgia, the George Durgins in Sacramento, California, my in-laws in Oklahoma and California, others at Grand Canyon, and then back to Washington for a few final days with us. Needless to say, Darek enjoyed it. Later, he went on to college and entered the Polish diplomatic service. He is now stationed in Lisbon as a foreign service officer. We still correspond with him and saw him recently on a trip to Portugal. Meanwhile, Jan has been to see us as well.

But it is my fellow ex-prisoners who we see most often, at reunions and on trips around the country. About half of them have now passed on. For the rest, I value their friendship and admire their fortitude, which I now suspect stems in large part from the Great Depression of the long-gone 1930s.

German POW Camps
in WWII

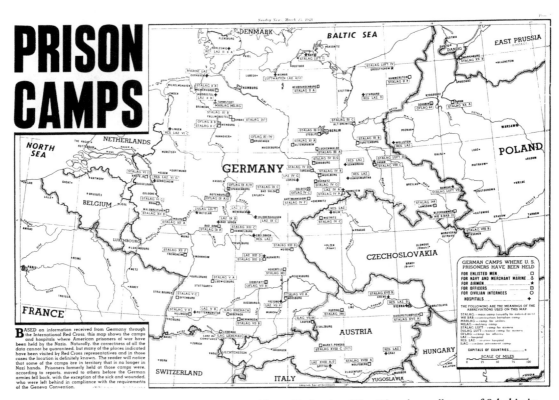

A map of the German prisoner of war camps in World War II, showing Oflag 64 at the small town of Schubin in northern Poland.

Highlights of the Geneva Convention

REGARDING THE TREATMENT OF PRISONERS OF WAR

APPENDIX **B**

Here, in basic English, are the highlights of the the 82 articles in the 1929 Geneva Convention, signed by both Germany and the United States, that deal with treatment of prisoners of war:

Article 2—Prisoners must be treated humanely and protected against acts of violence, insults and public curiosity. Measures of reprisal against them are prohibited.

Article 5—Every prisoner is required to give his name and rank, or else his regimental number. No coercion may be used on prisoners to secure information. Prisoners who refuse to answer may not be threatened, insulted or exposed to unpleasant or disadvantageous treatment.

Article 7—POWs shall be moved out of the combat zone as soon as possible to a rear area to be out of danger.

Article 10—Prisoners must be lodged in buildings or barracks affording all possible guarantees of hygiene and healthfulness. The quarters must be fully protected from dampness, sufficiently heated and lighted.

Article 11—The food ration of prisoners of war shall be equal in quantity and quality to that of troops at base camps. A sufficiency of potable water shall be furnished them as well.

Article 12—Clothing, linen and footwear shall be furnished to all prisoners of war by the detaining power. Replacement and repairing of these effects must be assured regularly.

Article 14—Every camp shall have an infirmary where prisoners shall receive every kind of attention they need.

Article 15—Medical inspections of prisoners of war shall be carried out at least once a month.

Article 27—Belligerents may utilize the labor of able prisoners of war according to their rank and aptitude. Officers and persons of equivalent status are excepted. Non-commissioned officers shall only be required to do supervisory work, unless they expressly request a remunerative occupation.

Article 36—Each belligerent shall periodically determine the number of letters and postcards which prisoners of various classes shall be allowed to send every month. Within a month of his capture every prisoner will be permitted to send his family a postal card telling of his capture and the state of his health.

Article 37—Each prisoner shall be allowed to receive parcels by mail, containing food or clothing.

Article 39—Prisoners of war shall be allowed to receive shipments of books individually.

Article 50—Escaped prisoners of war who are retaken before being able to rejoin their own army shall be liable only to disciplinary punishment.

Article 54—Arrest is the most severe disciplinary punishment which may be imposed on a prisoner of war. The duration of a single punishment may not exceed thirty days.

Article 56—Prisoners being punished shall be enabled to keep themselves in a state of cleanliness. They shall every day be allowed to exercise or stay in the open air at least two hours.

Article 77—Within the shortest possible period, each of the belligerent powers shall inform its information bureau of every capture of prisoners, giving it all the information regarding identity which it has, allowing it to quickly advise the families concerned and informing it of the address to which families may write to the prisoners.

Article 78—Relief societies for prisoners of war which are properly constituted with the object of serving as the channel for charitable effort, shall receive every facility for the efficient performance of their humane task within the bounds imposed by military necessities. Agents of these societies may be admitted to the camps for the purpose of distributing relief.

The Germans adhered to this agreement in dealing with their American prisoners of war most of the time in the early days of our involvement in the war, but violated it frequently and flagrantly as the war reached its climax.

The Oflag Item of October 1944

APPENDIX C

This is one fairly typical issue of our camp monthly paper, *The Item*, a six-pager for October 1944. It featured the winners of a picture contest of "The Gals We Left Behind" and a long addition to the monthly Oflag Directory— names and addresses of camp prisoners which came in handy after the war. The lead story reported the forthcoming, very successful three-act musical comedy, "Full Swing," written by two talented kriegies and produced that fall. There were plans for an extensive sports program in the fall, too, including boxing, deck tennis, wrestling, handball, soccer and football.

The Oflag 64 Item

FRAU EDITION　　　　　　**FRAU EDITION**

"One ITEM is Worth 10,000 Pictures"

No. 12　　　　　Altburgund, Germany — October 1, 1944　　　　　Price: 50 Pfg.

The Gals We Left Behind...

Nancy Reid, winner of the ITEM Picture Contest.

Marie Benzel, 2nd place

Clare Van Syckle, 3rd place

Oflag's First All-Original Show To Open Fall Entertainment Program

Illinois Beauty Wins Item Picture Contest

Nancy Reid, of Evanston, Ill., personal property of Lt. John Glendinning, is the beauteous winner of THE ITEM'S Gal Picture Contest.

A close second is Marie Benzel, left behind by Capt. Paul Miller, once of Lincoln, Nebr.

Gorgeous winner of third place is Dick Van Syckle's wife Clare.

In case there are any questions, the distinguished, well-qualified judges were Col. George Millett, Major Jerry Sage, and Lt. Tom Mitchell.

Other winners are pictured on page six.

OFLAG NEWS ● IN BRIEF ●

● After six months of constant appeals for pictures from home, Capt. Dick Rossbach was finally successful. He just received a snapshot of part of the apartment house in which he lives, and the back end of somebody else's car, sitting at an approximate angle of 45 degrees.

● Keith "Romeo" Willis has received one of the hottest of cupid's messages yet written to a kriegy. The young lady is unknown to him, unfortunately.

● Sid "Mouse" Waldman is now a big real estate operator. In a recent letter from his spouse, he finds he is the proud owner of a fifteen thousand dollar home. But he is still quartered in a bottom bunk of Zimmer 28.

● Boxing classes have now been opened to all bridge players. Two of the latest applicants come from barracks 8A.

● An article in the Oflag Daily Bulletin last month aroused such ire in the breast of a Barracks 7B stalwart, that he went around accusing all Texans within reach of being war profiteers.

● James Shoaf III has just joined the new car owner ranks of the camp with a sixteen hundred dollar Hudson. Ford, Diggs and Durgin, (and a good many others who are keeping it quiet) have found a friend indeed.

"Man Who Came To Dinner" Returns

Timed to open the fall theater program, the Oflag's first all-original show will hit the Little Theater on October 26.

"Full Swing," a three-act musical comedy written and produced by Dick Van Syckle and Larry Phelan, has original music by Vic Danylik, Sammy Saxton and Jack Cook.

The show will star Russ Ford, supported by Len Vaden, Dick Rossbach, Craig Campbell, Al Bohny, Frank Maxwell, Fred Somers, Jim Koch, Jack Cook, Carl Borrows, Don Waful and Howard Holder.

Scheduled for a five-day run starting October 12th is a revival of Jim Koch's spring success, "The Man Who Came to Dinner" with the original cast and new sets, costumes and props.

In the serious vein, Tom Holt will give his second operatic concert on October 20 and 21st, accompanied by Sammy Saxton.

Also scheduled for the month is a Swingland concert for five nights starting tonight.

New Sports Stars Appear

Late arrivals Bernie Goldman, Tom Murphy, Whit Whitfield, Don Graul, Bill Everett and Jim Weekly of the Barracks 7 softball and basketball teams bolster the Oflag's athletic front.

Whitfield and Graul formerly performed for semi-pro fives and Murphy was a member of the Westminister College Cagers. Goldman, who was looked over by Pittsburgh's Pirates, and Weekly played semi-pro baseball around Pittsburgh.

Something Different Today

After viewing the menu for 15 minutes, one of the new officers was heard to remark, "Good God! Nothing but soup today for dinner!"

TIME STAGGERS ON

As it must to all kriegies, hope came this week to time-marking, soup-eating, double-ugly Gefangener Gus, who had thought some day war would end. No pessimist, he.

To Gus, war and redcrossboxes were one. Now with but one week's supply, it followed war must fold.

Said Gus "No boxes, no war." Maybe.

The Oflag 64 Item

Published monthly by and for American officers temporarily detained in Offizierslager 64, Altburgnnd (Schubin), Germany.

Editor: 2nd Lt. Frank Diggs

Associate Editors: 1st Lt. Larry Phelan, 1st Lt. Willard Duckworth.

News: 2nd Lt. Frank Hancock.
    2nd Lt. Howard Holder
    2nd Lt. Frank Maxwell

Sports: 2nd Lt. Robert Cheatham

Art: 1st Lt. James Bickers, 2nd Lt. Alexander Ross

OCTOBER 1, 1944

«« ITEMIZING »»

We want to go on record as being only luke-warm toward the grandfather clock which has set itself up in the main building dispensing time in competition with all these nifty new Rolexes.

To begin with, we pre-expended Oflagites already have entirely too damn much time on our hands.

For instance, we've already served collectively something like five hundred years in this glorified hoosegow, and we don't like being reminded of it so much.

Then, too, grandfather ticks away deliberately in a tone of voice that says: "No rush, no rush."

Whereas those slick little Rolexes whisper shrilly "Let's get going-let's get going."

We second the motion. We think it's high time we got back to the eager young ladies on the front and back pages of this issue, who are doing a little clock-watching of their own.

Scotch Takes 2nd Place In Post-War Plans

Kriegies are the greatest dreamers in the world.

Now they have become more practical, to hell with the FAR future. How about that first moment of freedom?

Lt. Col. Schaefer, we understand, will make straight for a hidden cache of Scotch. He will use cover and concealment all the way to shake off any human parasites.

Lt. Red Banker will storm the Yale Club and order eight steaks two inches thick, a bushel of French fries and three quarts of milk.

Capt. John Peyton will hie to the nearest Walgreens and issue a field order for immediate action on a quadruple chocolate malted.

And Lt. Col. Gershenow... well we couldn't get much out of him. He merely said:

"Taking off my pack is the second thing I'll do."

RETROSPECT

By: Willard Duckworth

Looking back across the endless months
Of isolation from the outside world
  and untold boredom...
Petty selfishness... gray, introspective thought...
Vain dreams of a country bounded by two seas
Whose visions faded with the wash of Time
Until their moments of dazzling clarity
Darkened to elusive shades...

Remembering Kriegy evenings... soft... desolate... cold... bleak
(Countless now)
When the same old sun
(Although he sometimes changed his face and temperament)
Dropped from sight into a longed-for West
Patterned by a reach
Of rusty, jagged wire... eyes eternally watching it...
Trying to reckon on the times
That "when" was asked and "How long"...

What kept the mind and heart together
Through it all?
Secured each man's identity to himself
Lest blind desolation rip it from his grasp?
Simple words... forsaken... overlooked...
The same which guided Columbus to his shore.
Pluck Life from the with'ring touch of Death...
Halted floods... lifted famines...
Won wars and will win...

Enough. There is no riddle. You know as well as I
What bright flame has held you to the path...
And even now flares up to light
The whole, wide world.

In Sheep's Clothes...

"I say, Lieutenant, your stay in Germany didn't affect you any, did it?"

Kriegy Sketches

LT. LOUIS OTTERBEIN

Chief Carpenter and handiest man in camp is 6-foot Paratrooper Lou Otterbein of Bloomfield, N.J., who can do anything with a Klim tin except make it talk.

The man who built the stage of the Oflag Little Theater and who is responsible for most of the sets, furniture, props, and sound effects for the productions of the past year, was a big pigskin operator in pre-war days.

In 1935 he was capt. of Bloomfield's unbeaten, untied and unscored upon eleven and was All-Metropolitan center for New York and New Jersey that year. He received the Upson Memorial Scholarship to Rutgers where he played on the freshman team.

Lou got his jump training and his commission at Fort Benning where he had been a G.I. with the famed 29th Infantry. For him the war was over on July 10th last year when he jumped into the bag in Sicily.

Lou has a wife and two children waiting for him but is pessimistic about seeing them. He expects things to drag on for two weeks or more.

Air-corps Eyeview of Altburgund Academy

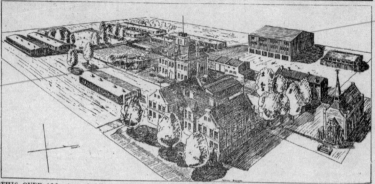

THIS OVER-ALL view of Oflag 64 by Staff Artist Jim Bickers is reprinted by general request.

OFLAG DIRECTORY

Continued from previous issues

ALABAMA
Carey Demott
2930 Dartmouth Ave., Bessemer

ARIZONA
James Carpenter
227 North Mount Vernon St., Prescott
Preston Hogue
2249 E. 2nd St., Tucson

CALIFORNIA
Peter Gaich
525 N. Kingsley Drive, Los Angeles
James Hannon
574 N. Sunnyslope, Pasadena
Paul Johnston
4760 Idaho St., San Diego
James MacIsaac
39 S. Kalorama St., Ventura
Donald Roberts
5043 Mount Royal Drive, Los Angeles
Patrick Teel
1837 N. Alexandria Ave., Hollywood
Osie Turner
Rt. 2, Box 113-B, Escalon
Herman Volbeim
710 Superba Ave., Venice
Howard Wallis
Rt. 1, Box 648, Denair

COLORADO
Patrick Trainor
Ordway

CONNECTICUT
Rudolph Malchiodi
29 High St., Deep River
Nicholas Rahal
8 Chichester Place, Danbury

DISTRICT OF COLUMBIA
Harvey Ford
2511 Que St., N.W., Washington
James Godfrey, Jr.
2505 13th St., N.W., Washington

Max Gooler
The Adjutant General, Washington
Marcellus Hughes
3808 Alton Place, N.W., Washington
Donald May
2208 Wyoming Ave., N.W.,
Washington 8
Clarence Melteson
4211 River Road, N.W., Washington
Louis Morgenrath
1210 – 12th St., N.W., Washington
Alfred Moss
The Adjutant General, Washington
John Waters
3900 Tunlaw Road, N.W., Washington 7

GEORGIA
Collins Kendrick, Jr.
374 Orange St., Macon
Arthur Mallory
LaGrange
William Shuler, J.
1007 2nd Ave., Albany

IDAHO
Reid Ellsworth
166 Taft Ave., Pocatello
Kenneth Speas
Shelley

ILLINOIS
William Cool
343 West Censer St., Paxton
Thomas Johnson
502 Greenwood Av., Kenilworth
Tom MaGee
912 So. 3rd St., Springfield
Owen McGee
1405 S. Euclid, Chicago
James Schmitz
804 Illinois Ave., Ottawa

INDIANA
Francis Habig
1105 No. Main St., Jasper
Carl Kasper
1210 Condit St., Hunting'on
William Morris
4325 Winthrop Ave., Indianapolis

IOWA
Richard Davis
10 Achre Apts, Fort Dodge
Duane Smith
General Delivery, Colfax

KANSAS
Norman Alloway
Rt. 1, Edna
James Ralstin
5639 West Maple, Wichita

KENTUCKY
James Dew
Calvert City
Robert Watt, Jr.
Tates Creek Pike, Lexington

LOUISIANA
Howard Charlton
1366 Scenic Highway, Baton Rouge
Peter Graffagnino
2814 S. Carrollton Ave., New Orleans
Harry Picou
Montegut Rte., Houma

MARYLAND
William Bond
406 American Bldg, Baltimore
Martin Upperco
706 Oldhome Rd., Raspeburg

MASSACHUSETTS
Edward Humphrey
Rochester

DIRECTORY (Continued)

George Maibach
49 Tyler St., N. Quincy

Thomas Miller, Jr.
5 Gould Ave., East Walpole

John O'Neil
36 Tufts St., Medford

Michael Piecuch
11 Atwood St., Newburyport

Alfred Reid
45 Belmont Street, Cambridge

MICHIGAN

Lewis Bixby
26044 Dundee Rd., Royal Oak

Jeremiah Moher
14910 Southampton, Detroit

Arnold Perkins
422 W. Green St., Hastings

Stanley Peters
12079 Jennings Rd., Clio

Frederick Saam
Calumet

Donald Wernette
Mecosta

MISSISSIPPI

Edward Kitchens
Kings Daughters Hospital, Greenville

MISSOURI

James Berry
Knobnoster

Wilbur Fulkerson
Coffey

Myrl Hodson
2008 Poplar Ave., Kansas City

Wayne Immekus
6529 San Bonita, Clayton

William Reno
2605 Benton Blvd., Kansas City

MINNESOTA

Gordon Berg
New Richland

Clarence Dutkowski
308 5th Ave., NE, Brainerd

Donald Hemler
4916 Ewing Ave., S. Minneapolis

Arthur LeSage, Jr.
Rt. 1, Morris

NEBRASKA

Keneth Gingrich
Riverton

Lynn Hunsaker
Auburn

Paul Miller
1729 K St., Lincoln

NEW HAMPSHIRE

Anthony Chrzanowski
Pellham Road, Hudson

Robert Crandall
Northwood Narrows

NEW JERSEY

Alfred Bolny
High View Drive, Wyckoff

James Larkin
336 Broad Ave., Englewood

Anthony Sito
407½ So. 11th St., Newark

NORTH CAROLINA

John Dimling, Jr.
701 Oaklawn Ave., Winston-Salem

John Dobson
820 Country Club Dr., Greensboro

NEW YORK

Ralph Gaun
1732 Ave. "A", Schenectady

Harold Houghton
Parish

James Jordan
767 E. Main St., Little Falls

Robert Kramer
229 E. 85th St., New York

Maurice Topping
1607 Prospect Pl., Brooklyn

Justin Ware
87 Bedford St., New York

OREGON

Raymond Steinke
1873 Court St., Salem

PENSYLVANIA

Carl Hunsinger
353 Lightstreet Rd., Bloomsburg

George Oughton
5513 Marshall St., Philadelphia

Theodore Pawloski
850 Shoemaker Ave., West Wyoming

Charles Palumbo
3126 F. St., Philadelphia

John Slack
1220 Filmore St., Philadelpia

Edgar Spicher
Pleasant Gap

Sidney Thal
4130 Girard Ave., Philadelphia

William Ullery
712 2nd St., Brownsville

John Vargo
38 Vine St., Lancaster

Robert Wick
Bradford

Albert Winwood
7725 Cannon St., Swissvale

Oflag Strength Jumps as 101 Arrive in September

New arrivals here this month include: Lt. Cols. E.A. Cummings, E. G. Hardaway, W. G. Hopkins, Jr.; Majors G. M. Simes, G.K. Smith; Capts. E. Anthony, W.W. Bishop, A.O. Dyroff, J.T. Eichnor, H.D. Eldridge, J.P. Forsyth, J.N.Harris, O.C. Hart, F.C. Healy, L.L. Moore, W.W. Paty, Jr., W.L. Schoener, T. V. Sigler, R.J. Smith, B.C. Swaim, W.R.Sweeney; 1st Lts. R. N. Alday, B. V. Amato, G.R. Barfoot, A. R. Blanchard, S. A. Bradley, C. H. Brown, D. E. Brown, L. A. Brown, H. H. Bush, S. Curlick, J. W. Carlson, H. P. Claus, J. H. Doran, H. L. Garris, W. R. Harrell, E. P. Harrison, P. W. Hodnette, B. E. Kleber, Leon E. Lavender, W.R. Lee, J.B. Mattingly, J. E. Mazoroff, M.N. McArthur, J.B.McDonald, E. L. Miller, I. R. Miller, T. O. Morton, J. J. O'Connor, Jr., R.W. Oker, H.M.Pike, H.V. Richard, J.A. Rightley, J.H.Rogers, G. Seeman, T. W. Silva, R. D. Tedeschi, E.M. Vinson,P.B.Ward,O.R.Williams,Jr., O. T. Ziegler; 2nd Lts. A. G. Alderton, S.Bacchus, Jr., S. Bailin, W.H. Beemer, C.G. Bedient,*F.J. Bova, J.L.Boyd, H.J. Carroll, C.F. Clawson, G.L.Daubenspeck, J.N. Fahey, J.T. Feilen, E.A. Graf, G. I. Greene, S. Gwosden, C.F. Hansen, H.W. Hayes, R.D.Heil, J.F. Hinchcliffe, R.E. Holmquist, R.L. Jenkins, O.K. Kirkpatrick, D. B. Lott, P. D. McIntyre, H. J. O'Connor, F. C. Ostrander, G. B. Powell, C. Scherer, S.J. Segal, L. L. V. Smith, W.W.Smith, N.H. Spitzer, C.M. Stocker, C. F. Sullivan, Jr., R. L. Whiteturkey, D. G. Williams, H. J. Wright, F.W. Dingledine, and D. B. Streett.

Altburgund Skyline...

OFLAG SPORTS

Soccer, Football Head Extensive Fall Sports Program, Planned by New 15-Man Oflag Recreation Staff

SPORTS SIDELIGHTS
By: Robert Cheatham

Retiring 21 consecutive batters, Major Jerry Sage pitched the Oflag's first perfect game, a 9-0 victory over "Hot" Cool's team last month in the camp softball league.

While his club scored nine runs on 12 hits and opponent's miscues, the blonde major allowed no hits, no walks and received perfect support to keep Cool's batters from reaching first base.

Focal point of enlisted men's sports activities has shifted to the basketball court after three months on the diamond. Ferguson, Herrington and Lescanec, ex-high school and semi-pro performers, stand out in spirited after-appell games.

Exhibition basketball games between barracks, initiated last month, will continue each Saturday throughout the fall according to court mentor Bob Bonner.

Paced by Bill Luttrell's Room 9 team, the select teams offer fast tilts for kriegy kabitzers.

Jottings...

Lee LeClaire, American Legion forward dropped three shots through the hoop, to score 6 points in 30 seconds against the YMCA quintet... Whit Whitfield racked up 24 points in his first game in gefangenshaft... Don May's volleyball squad required an hour and 45 minutes to lick Bill Farrell's team in the season's longest two-game match... "Leaping Leebo" Lee, internationally famous trick shot artist, performs daily on the local basketball court... Long John Scully played his first basketball here last summer... Davis to Soliday to Moller doubled Kent off second, Sims off first and put out batter Lohrenga!, who had lined to Davis in shortfield to start the ball rolling. for the fourth triple play in the camp softball league!!!

New Sports Program Includes Boxing, Deck Tennis, Wrestling, Handball

Indoor and outdoor sports designed for participation by every officer are planned for the fall and winter season by Major John Dobson, newly-appointed camp recreation officer.

Soccer and touch-football leagues will begin play at the end of the current softball schedule, while basketball will continue under the present set-up.

Nice Work

For doing a swell job in directing the Oflag sports program, THE ITEM awards the official Block "S" to retiring Athletics Officer Herb Johnson, and assistants Leo Farber, Bob Bonner and Ed Spicher.

Johnson became sports director in July, '43, while Farber, Spicher and Bonner have been in charge of the three major sports throughout the summer.

Barracks Three Wins '44 Oflag Olympics

Jerry Long's Barracks "3" squad scored 49 points to win the fastest relays (outside of God's country) since the '36 Olympic, at the Althurgund Track and Field Meet, held here last month.

The White House took second place with 39 points followed by Barracks "6", Barracks "8", 21 and Barracks "7", 17.

Ellsworth Cundiff, Barracks "3" 's ex-collegiate star, chalked up 13 points with two first and one second place to win high-scoring honors. Another "3" star, John Shirk, was runner-up with 8½ points.

Plans for the indoor season include chess, ping-pong and bridge tournaments and a chess ladder.

The new sports staff is:

Maj. J.W. Dobson	Sports Officer
Capt. W.R. Bond	Assistant
Lt. W.E. Evans	Basketball
Lt. W.W. Luttrel	Touch Football
Lt. R.L. Marnien	Soccer
Capt. D.L. May	Volleyball
Lt. J.W. Banker	Wrestling
Lt. P.A. Teel	Boxing
Lt. J.J. Hasson	Gymnasium
Lt. J.J. Hasson	Ping-Pong
Lt.Col. H.W. Sweeting	Chess
Lt. J.L. Cockrell	Bridge
Lt. G. Long	Golf
Maj. M.A. Meacham	Deck Tennis
Lt. H.A. Casner	Handball

John Creech, Leo Farber and Cundiff turned in top records of the meet in winning the cross-country, 100-Yd. dash and high jump events.

Geprüft: Oflag 64, Abteilung I'd. Druck: Willi Kricks, Altburgund

Prison Daze...   By: Bickers

The Gals We'd Like To Go Home To...

HERE ARE SIX of the Oflag's smoothest gefangen-widows, greatly admired by the ITEM'S Picture Contest judges. (SEE PAGE ONE) They are: TOP (L) Helen Moore, Kemp, Texas; (R)Mary Louise Falls, Oakland City, Ind: MIDDLE (L) Carolyn McDonald, Albany, N. Y.; (R) Neenie Miller, Fort Knox, Ky.; BOTTOM (L) Myrtle Polson, Creston, Iowa; (R) Gladys Graham, Wilkinburg, Pa. (who won 4th place).

Soederberg's Farewell

APPENDIX

DHenry Soederberg, probably the best benefactor of the American prisoners at Oflag 64, was unwell in 1997 and did not expect to attend the annual reunion at Newport, Rhode Island. So he wrote a final message to be read to the group there. As it turned out, he did attend the reunion, but died a month later. This is a copy of his last, unread message to the surviving kriegies:

Dear Oflag 64 friends,

Only circumstances and events completely outside my control have prevented me from participating in your reunion. This time I was firmly set to come and had very much been looking forward to once more be with you.

It has been said that this is your last reunion. In a way, from a formal and official point of view, this may be true. However, I am convinced that as long as there are living members of this great group you will continue to congregate—in one way or another—until there is only one left of you. [*Actually, the reunions have continued on since then.*]

As prisoners during World War II you played a significant role. You endured hardship and brutality with dignity and with determination to live on. You never gave up. You used your time behind the wires to improve your knowledge and increase your common sense. And you learned how important it is to be considerate and understanding of the needs of others and to share with them your own limited resources, including space. You also learned how important small and simple things could become as the basis for dignified living: a soap, a toilet paper, a razor blade, a piece of paper, a pencil, a book, and so on. You also found that time is an important capital which can be profitably used when there is a will to survive and to plan and prepare for the future. You also found out that physical and mental occupation is necessary in order to sustain healthy living. Above all, you learned during your time as prisoners to treasure freedom.

As a former delegate of the War Prisoners Aid of the YMCA, I am happy every time I get evidence that our work—which was concentrated on just the small basic needs of your daily life—in many cases could help prisoners to achieve some of the values that made life worth living. The Y services were in a way complimentary necessities; they were also a reminder that you were not forgotten by people outside the prison camp. Hundreds of thousands of people, your relatives and friends, and countless other persons who did not know you personally contributed to the Y work because they simply felt they had to assist in an important task.

I have told you time after time how happy and grateful I am that I was given the opportunity to serve the prisoners of war. Believe me, this was not a sacrifice for me. On the contrary, it was a great challenge and, to a young man, a great adventure. The contacts I made during the war have continued over the years and developed into a friendship of a special kind. I regard these friendships as something of the best thing given to me in my lifetime.

Some ex-POW friends have asked me, out of curiosity, how much money we were paid by the YMCA for our work and if we got some retirement benefits when the war was over. This may be a fitting question today when the world is full of "professional" delegates of hundreds of organizations often paid with government money. The salaries of the Y delegates were related to their civic and social situation at home. As a rule, a delegate should have a salary identical to what he had at home, with allowances for children and responsibilities. Fresh out of university and without a firm income, I got about $70 a month, a good salary in my opinion. The money went to bank accounts or dependents directly. All of my immediate living costs while working, traveling, and living in Germany went on expense account. (There was really nothing to buy!) Our directives were to live as comfortably as possible in order to gather strength for the visits to POW camps. As time went on, the possibilities for "luxury living" in Hitler's Germany were nil. On journeys we had to sleep wherever we found a bed or bench. The food provided in restaurants was meager. Like you, we could keep alive thanks to parcels sent from the Red Cross or from home. Of course when we stayed for some days at our German head office in Berlin or Sagan we could experience a more homelike atmosphere, but even there comfortable living came to an end. For the last four months of the war, each delegate had to live on his own and improvise his living and work in all respects. Several of us ended up in POW camps ourselves; it was then more safe inside the wires than outside.

For those of us who had volunteered for the war service, there were no postwar compensations or pensions whatsoever, something which we understood from the start. However, the YMCA paid a life insurance policy for us. In my case, being young, with no firm position at home, and no family or dependents apart from my parents, it amounted to the staggering amount of $3,000, or roughly one year's salary, according to the exchange rate. But at that time, of course, the value was much higher, though not staggering.

No, we did not get rich moneywise. But I treasure more than anything else those four years that I spent in the work for prisoners. The elderly gentlemen who were running the whole YMCA operation during the war were experienced and wise. They used to say: "This work will never make you rich. But after the war you will feel the gratefulness and friendship of those you served and this will mean much more than any monetary compensation." And this is just how I have experienced it at the meetings with you and ex-POWs from other camps during the whole postwar period.

Much more could be said on this occasion, but I shall end here with many thanks to all of you for the friendship and comradeship you have showed to me over the years. It has been a great source of inspiration. My special thanks go to those of you with whom I was able to establish more personal contacts with our families involved. I cannot enumerate you all but I am thinking especially of people (dead or alive) like the Drakes, the Burgesons, the Waters, the Slacks, the Diggs, the Holders, the Garrets, and so on.

Please let me know when and where the next reunion will take place since I am sure there will be another.

My wife, Claire, whom I met when I worked for you in Germany, also worked for you both behind the stage in Germany and Geneva. She sends her best regards to you all.

Affectionately and in everlasting friendship,

Henry Soederberg

The *Oflag 64 Bulletin*

E

The Daily Bulletins Come Home

Our wall newspaper, known as *The Daily Bulletin*, turned out to be an important morale factor at Oflag 64 in keeping everybody informed daily on how the war was going, what the Germans were reporting about it, and on activities within the camp. There were 250 postings altogether, each the size of an American newspaper front page. We hoped that there would be some way of getting them home after the war. Just in case, the camp bookbindery put most of them into two bound volumes, each about two inches thick and quite heavy.

There was no way, of course, for such big bound volumes of newspapers to be carried out on the long, grueling march back to Germany when the camp was evacuated in January, 1945. But our ace staff member, Lt. Seymour Bolten, who spoke German and some Russian, was left behind to help the 85 sick or wounded kriegies who remained in the camp in the hopes that they would be rescued by the oncoming Russians. Seymour agreed to try and bring the thick bound volumes out if the Russians trucked the group of sick and wounded prisoners out to Russia and eventually home.

The Russians did indeed show up, did not shoot up the camp (as some predicted), and eventually provided a convoy of American-made trucks to carry the hospital group out of the camp and across Poland—but not to Russia. Seymour managed to smuggle the two volumes of *Daily Bulletins* aboard one of the trucks, which delivered the American group to the refugee camp at Rembertov, just outside of Warsaw.

There I met up with the group, having been lucky enough to escape from the marching column and hitchhike across Poland to the same refugee center. Seymour and I agreed to try to carry the heavy volumes as far as we could on our uncertain travels in the direction of home. It wasn't easy, but we did lug the bound volumes aboard the box car that in due time carried our group of ex-kriegies across Russia to Odessa. From here we lugged them aboard a British ship to Egypt, then to Naples and eventually squeezed them into a crowded stateroom in a troop ship back to Boston.

After the war, the two volumes rested for some time in my various civilian attics, surfacing from time to time at kriegy reunions. Then word of their existence reached the Army and they were requested by the U.S. Army Military History Institute, located on the campus of the Army War College in Carlisle Barracks, Pennsylvania. There they now reside, along with a growing collection of books and memorabilia concerning Oflag 64 in World War II.

Following in this Appendix are examples of some of the reproducible issues of *The Daily Bulletin* which are now on file at the Institute. They were photographed in mid–1999 by Gerhard Dreo.

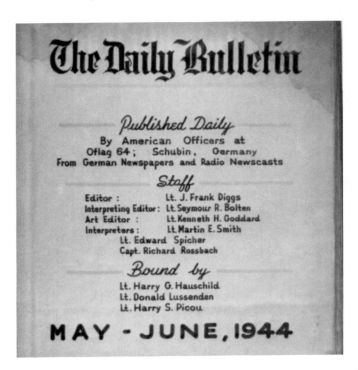

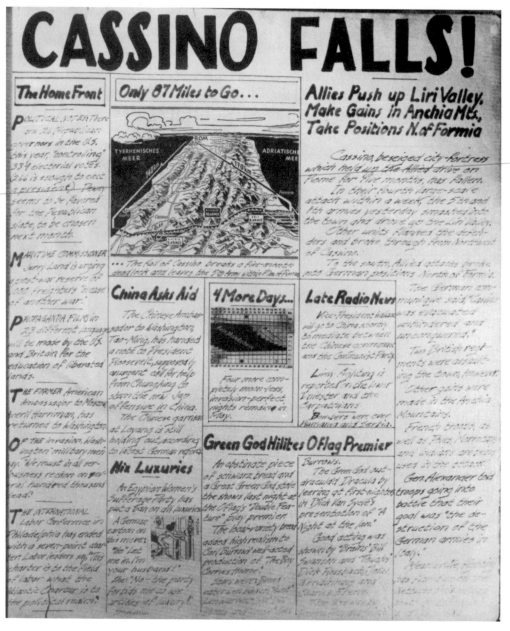

The big news in the 19 May 1944 issue of the *Daily Bulletin* was the fall of Cassino. The German defense of Cassino had held up the Allied drive up the Italian Peninsula for 5 months. Interest in a review of the latest Oflag 64 play, however, was a close second.

ITALIAN PINCERS TIGHTEN

The Home Front...

Pres. Roosevelt Plans World Confederation

'Human Torpedo'...

Canadian Corps Hits Roccasecca On Right Flank

...This gadget is an Italian 2-man human torpedo. You steer it toward a ship and then jump quick. It may be used against invasion ships.

Pass the Fish-heads, Mr. Moto

Secondary Front

The Fine Art of Bombing the Third Reich

On 30 May 1944, the German press admitted that the allies were tightening their pincers in Italy and stepping up the bombing in Germany. The drawing under the heading, "The Fine Art of Bombing the Third Reich" was from a German publication.

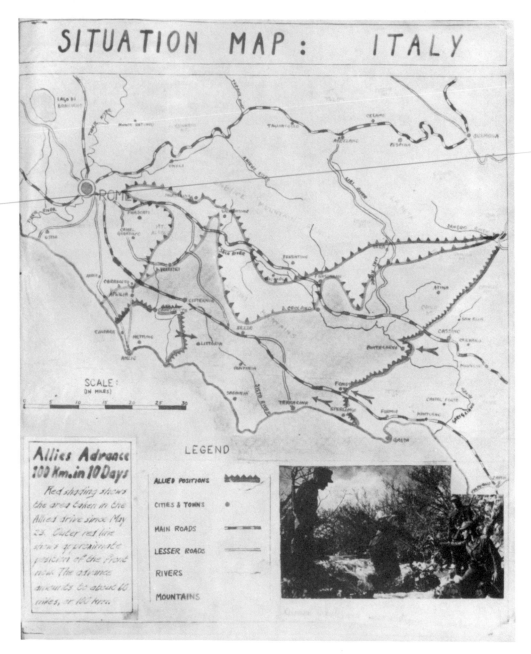

The German press was now providing war data in unusual detail concerning Italy—enough to allow us to provide this map of recent allied advances to our readers.

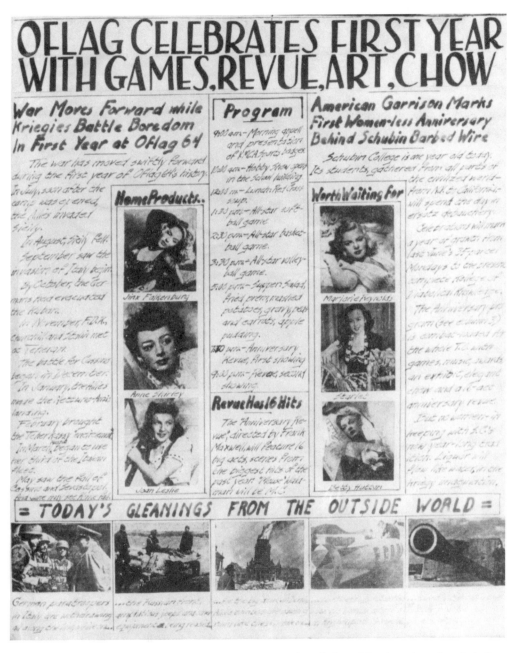

On 05 June 1944, the eve of D-Day, the *Daily Bulletin* reported on the big celebration, planned weeks before, of the camps first anniversary.

In our October 18, 1944 issue, the *Daily Bulletin* had kind words for the late Field Marshal Erwin Rommel, while reporting that *Time* predicted that Germany faced the fate of Carthage.

As the November elections neared in the United States, a newly arrived kriegy provided us with a copy of the overseas ballots being sent to troops in Europe. We were also pleased to learn that the invasion of the Philippines was underway.

ELECTION CAMPAIGN NEARS END

Presidential Race Is Quiet

"Gloriously defeated..."

F.D.R. with adviser Bernard Baruch

On November 7, the voters of America will go to the polls to elect their president for a new 4-year term after one of the quietest election campaigns in many years.

With the nation absorbed by the tasks of global war, the candidates have made no attempt at intensive electioneering.

President Roosevelt has made several speeches on the progress of the war, while candidate Dewey has attacked F.D.R's handling of the war effort.

The campaign's only excitement occurred at the Democratic Convention when Vice President Henry A. Wallace made a strong and dramatic but ineffective bid to secure the renomination.

The youngest Republican presidential candidate in many campaigns is Thomas E. Dewey, Governor of New York State. Dewey first achieved fame as "racket-buster" in New York City where he was special prosecutor by appointment of the then Governor, Herbert Lehman. He promises, if elected president, to effect economies in the government and return the country to "old-fashioned Americanism".

Dewey's running-mate is "Honest John" Bricker, Governor of the state of Ohio since 1939. Bricker has been non-committal in his campaign speeches on his proposed policies if elected Vice President. His claim to the office is based chiefly on his record of an efficient and economical administration in his home state.

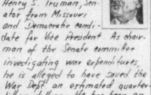

One of the key figures in the war effort back home is Henry S. Truman, Senator from Missouri and Democratic candidate for Vice President. As chairman of the Senate committee investigating war expenditures, he is alleged to have saved the War Dept. an estimated quarter-billion dollars. He has been an unsparing critic of waste in the armed forces, and in war industry.

THE LAST ELECTIONS: "Grey states" went Democratic, and "white states" Republican in the state elections of 1943; states with ⓦ voted for Wendell Willkie in 1940.

Kriegies get a look at the forthcoming 1944 election back in the United States in this Feature Page devoted to the Roosevelt vs. Dewey race.

5th ANNIVERSARY OF WAR BRINGS END IN SIGHT

U.S. Forces Play Vital Role in Past Two Years of War

Today is the fifth Anniversary of the war.

Five years of war has brought the end in sight. The turning point was marked two years ago when Allied forces invaded North Africa.

Since then, mileposts of the Allied onslaught have been:

—1942—
Nov. 8: Invasion of Africa.

—1943—
May 1: Fall of Tunis.
May 13: End of the African campaign.
July 9: Invasion of Sicily.
July 24: Fall of Palermo.
Aug. 17: Messina evacuated— End of campaign.
Sept. 3: Invasion of Italy at Reggio.
Sept. 9: Capitulation of Italy.
Sept. 9: Landing at Salerno

—1944—
Jan. 22: Landing at Anzio.
May 18: Fall of Cassino.
June 5: Fall of Rome.
June 6: Invasion of North France (Normandy)
June 26: Fall of Cherbourg.
Aug. 15: Invasion of South France.
Aug. 23: Fall of Paris.
Sept. 1: Fall of Verdun and Amiens.
Sept. 3: Allied spearheads 33 miles from Belgium border, 55 miles from old German border.

① While strong Russian armored columns swept through German defenses from Stalingrad to Warsaw......

② Allied troops invaded and occupied North Africa. Then they..

③ captured the islands of Pantellaria and Sicily and landed in force on the Italian mainland

④ where they took Rome in a gigantic drive and pushed the Germans back to Northern Italy..

⑤ Then strong contingents of Air and Sea-borne troops hit the North and South coasts of France, penetrated strong coastal defenses

⑥ and pushed inland to liberate Paris after four years of German occupation. Armored spearheads are now striking East to Germany.

As the war approached its climax in Europe, another Feature Page gives the highlights of the conflict, year by year.

DEMOBILIZATION PLAN ANNOUNCED FOR YANKS AT END OF EUROPEAN WAR

Wedded To Go First

First-hand knowledge of a planned demobilization of approximately 2,000,000 members of the U.S. Armed Forces after the war is given by recent arrivals here, who quote "Stars and Stripes" as giving a "point discharge plan".

A "four point" system will determine who will be discharged first, and the lucky ones will be mostly from the E.T.O.

Married men who have had most overseas combat will leave first, most of the men discharged being enlisted men.

Rating Cards Planned

Briefly, this is how it will work: Soon after it is over over here, the Theater Commander will issue "adjusted service rating cards" on which will be scored these factors:

1. SERVICE CREDIT, based on total months of army service since Sept. 16, 1940.

2. OVERSEAS CREDIT, based on number of months overseas.

3. COMBAT SERVICE, based on awards to individuals, i.e. Purple Heart, etc.

4. PARENTHOOD CREDIT, which gives credit for each dependent child under 18, up to a limit of three.

Combat Credit Given

Value of points will not be announced until cessation of hostilities, but reliable sources indicate overseas credit will get 1 point for each month, service credit will get 1 point for each month, combat credit will be worth 5 points, and each dependent child will give eight points.

The plan will initially provide the biggest release of soldiers in the ground forces. In the case of officers, military necessity will determine who is non-essential. Officers will be released only as they can be spared.

Examples Shown

This is the way it works: Assume there are four infantry divisions in the European Theater of Operations. One of these divisions is unnecessary for fighting in the Pacific Theater, or for occupational police work in Europe.

On the basis of the credit cards and nature of their work, transfers will be made to "surplus divisions". Remaining men will be shifted to outfits earmarked for retention in Europe, or transfer to the Pacific Theater of Operations. Men in the surplus divisions will be returned to the States. When they arrive, they will go directly to surplus pools. From there they will be sent to "separation centers" nearest their homes, the men with most points leaving first.

It is believed that most officer personnel will be retained on active duty for a considerable period of time after the war.

CARTOON is by Staff Artist Jim Bickers.

INFORMATION was compiled by James Schmidt.

With the end of our time in Oflag 64 approaching, a new arrival appeared with a report on the Army's tentative plans for postwar demobilization. It was read very closely.

Index